male/female roles

1989 annual

David L. Bender, *Publisher*
Bruno Leone, *Executive Editor*
Bonnie Szumski, *Senior Editor*
Janelle Rohr, *Senior Editor*
Susan Bursell, *Editor*
William Dudley, *Editor*
Robert Anderson, *Assistant Editor*
Karin Swisher, *Assistant Editor*
Lisa Orr, *Assistant Editor*

greenhaven press, inc.

PO Box 289009
San Diego, CA 92128-9009

© 1989 by Greenhaven Press, Inc.

ISBN 0-89908-544-X
ISSN 0897-7372

contents

Editor's Note

Opposing Viewpoints SOURCES provide a wealth of opinions on important issues of the day. The annual supplements focus on the topics that continue to generate debate. Readers will find that *Opposing Viewpoints SOURCES* become the barometers of today's controversies. This is achieved in three ways. First, by expanding previous chapter topics. Second, by adding new materials which are timeless in nature. And third, by adding recent topical issues not dealt with in previous volumes or annuals.

Viewpoints

"The large family is the best preventive against the loneliness which is so all-pervasive in modern society."

Large Families Are Beneficial

Herbert Ratner

The difficulty in raising an only child is generally recognized. Parents find themselves without previous experience at child-rearing and without the salutary effect of siblings on the lone child.

In the face of preoccupation with the alleged "population explosion," where social engineers are urging limitation of family size to one or two children, by fiat if necessary, some prominent scientists (Rene Dubos and Erik Erikson, for example) have warned of the dangers of taking the small family as the norm for man. Erikson writes: "Just as sexual repression characterized the Victorian era, so repression of the urge to have children may characterize the future." Psychiatrists, he continues " . . . can easily overlook how much some modern persons who are practicing systematic birth control may need enlightenment in regard to what they are doing."

The elimination of larger families would short-circuit the rich diversity of the human race. There is not only the primary diversity of man at the genetic level, due to intermingling of chromosomes from the two sexes, there is also a secondary diversity which occurs through differences in family constellation. These are multitudinous, *viz.*, eldest, middle and youngest children develop different personalities traceable in considerable part to their relative position within the family.

One internationally recognized pediatrician (Sir James Spence, a Protestant who believes in birth control) argues for five children as the minimum family size necessary for the optimum rearing of children. My own belief is that the minimum optimum is three children. The third child sharply increases the probability that the children will not all be of one sex, thus better preparing siblings for

two-sexed society. Again, the third child protects against polarization along the lines of sex, age or dominance. Moreover, the third child dramatically multiplies and enriches the dynamics of family life.

"Little Emperors"

Consider the case of China's present arithmetical approach to "overpopulation"—the one-child family. Not being satisfied with the great headway it made educationally, which virtually eliminated premarital sex and postponed marriage age into the late twenties, it opted for the one-child family.

Had China consulted me on their problem, I would have said (as I did in 1982): "Better one family with five children than five families with one child each." But China hadn't consulted me. The returns of its experiment are now coming in. True, the size of the population is being reduced, but China is now producing a generation of "brats":

> Eight years after the world's most populous nation put its controversial family-planning program in effect, limiting most couples to one child, one of the most conspicuous results has been the rise of a generation of "little emperors," which in the West would be known as spoiled brats.
> Many only children are so doted upon by their families that they become timid, overbearing, lazy, self-indulgent or contemptuous of physical labor, officials said. . . .

> Newspapers constantly warn adults against indulging in the "4-2-1 syndrome," in which four grandparents and two parents pamper an only child. (*The Philadelphia Inquirer*, July 27, 1987)

> Peking, UPI—Doctors are concerned that China's "one couple, one child" family-planning policy is producing a generation of fat, spoiled children.
> According to the New China news agency, doctors are worried about the growing number of overweight youngsters, many of whom are pampered by their parents with calorie-packed goodies like chocolate, sugar and high-fat meat. (*The Chicago Tribune*, Jan. 28, 1986)

Herbert Ratner, "'Optimum' Family Size and the Value of Children," *A.L.L. About Issues*, August/September 1988. Reprinted with permission.

A more disturbing consideration, however, is the kind of society that will exist when the second generation of single children appear on the scene. These children will have no aunts, no uncles and no cousins. When their grandparents die and later their parents, they will have no blood relations, unless they marry and have a child of their own. If they don't marry, who among their relatives will be there to pray for them when they die? What a radical transformation of China's society! Does this foretell a move to a state-ruled animal colony?

And there is a further point to be made. Family counselors report that marriages of only children or eldest children are the most difficult. What will be the consequences?

The Value of Children

Young couples getting married today are nowhere more ignorant than in their failure to appreciate the significance of children in marriage. Family life programs, including Catholic programs, stand under special indictment for neglecting to inculcate in couples the gift, the pleasures and the value of children.

[Danish philosopher Soren] Kierkegaard said: "The trouble with life is that we understand it backwards but have to live it forwards." Our goal should be to educate the young so that they understand life as they live it forward and thereby help them make prudential judgments. The greatest regret of American married women toward the end of life is that they hadn't had a child or hadn't had more children. . . .

1. Children are a gift biologically as well as theologically. Man is a relatively sterile animal. Couples flock to birth control and family planning clinics in their twenties but switch to sterility clinics in the thirties. Babies for adoption are at a premium. Test-tube babies and surrogate mothers measure their plight.

2. The time-span from age 38 to age 58 or from age 58 to age 78 is no longer and no shorter than the span from age 18 to age 38. But that which gives pleasure in life tends to differ for the respective age groups. What seems more of a chore and intrusion in one's personal life when one is young becomes far less a chore and intrusion as one grows older.

Children become more and more important to a person with advancing age. The joys of grandparenthood are well known. Children are seen as a blessing where once they may have been viewed as a hardship. In countries with sharply reduced birth rates we are now hearing of the sufferings of a grandparentless society. Even death itself becomes more bearable when the dying are surrounded by loved ones. One does not go through life feeling always like a teenager or young adult, yet what one does in these earlier years may preclude the joys of later life.

Certainly God does not expect the young couple to embark on marriage preoccupied with grandparenthood and death, but God does expect a couple to avoid doing what would rob them of the happiness which should come with the later stages of life. In this context, couples should be attentive to the core principle of *Humanae Vitae*, of preserving the integral oneness of the unitive and procreative aspects of marriage. D.H. Lawrence makes the point poetically: "We are bleeding at the roots, because we are cut off from the earth and sun and stars, and love is a grinning mockery, because, poor blossom, we plucked it from its stem on the Tree of Life, and expected it to keep on blooming in our civilized vase on the table."

3. The choicest gift one can bequeath to a child is not material possessions but another brother or sister.

4. Parents do not live forever, and children have each other after their parents pass on. At family reunions the children, now uncles and aunts, have the opportunity to pass on family stories which give the grandchildren a sense of roots, of their unique heritage.

5. Children mature parents more than parents mature children. For most adults, parenthood is the road to maturity. It is capable of converting the selfish into the unselfish.

6. The large family is the best preventive against the loneliness which is so all-pervasive in modern society. One can go on. . . .

"The greatest regret of American married women toward the end of life is that they hadn't had a child or hadn't had more children."

Nature's prescription not only shortens the obligations of the pre-school period, (1) it brings youth to child-bearing and the arduous early child-rearing years, (2) it permits children to grow up with more intimately shared lives, (3) it closes the generation gap between parent and child, particularly valuable in the adolescent years, (4) it lengthens the joys of parenthood and grandparenthood, (5) it allows for leeway in case of obstetrical misfortunes and tragic events, (6) it gives parents the opportunity to reexamine their goals while reproductive options are still available, and (7) it rids the couple of the fear of an unplanned pregnancy with each love act, permitting them blissfully to ignore birth control for nine years or more during the period of greatest sexual activity.

Herbert Ratner is a medical doctor and editor of Child and Family Quarterly *in Oak Park, Illinois.*

One-Child Families Are Beneficial

Ann Garcelon

Almost immediately after the birth of her son in 1975, Sharryl Hawke, then 30, an educator and writer living in Boulder, Colorado, began to seriously consider having another baby.

"I didn't really want to have another child but I didn't want my son to be an only child, either. It wouldn't be fair to him, I thought, if he had to grow up without a brother or sister," she says. "I worried that he wouldn't grow up to be normal and well-balanced. What if we spoiled him? What if he grew up feeling lonely—or became too much of a loner?"

Sharryl worried so much about it that she became depressed. "My husband finally made me see that I was focusing on all the wrong issues—that we shouldn't have another child simply to prevent our son from being an 'only.' Eventually, after talking about it for months, we decided that one could be wonderful. And it has been."

Sharryl's son, Mark, now 15 years old, is a happy, well-adjusted child. And Sharryl has changed her mind about "onlys."

Common Beliefs

The beliefs she held are not uncommon. Many people think that the child who grows up without siblings is destined to become a socially handicapped adult who is selfish, egotistical, dependent and lonely.

Many people also think that the parents of an only child must either be experiencing infertility problems—and therefore are to be pitied—or they are just plain selfish.

More and more couples, however, have been questioning the wisdom, or lack of it, in such beliefs—as is evidenced by the growing number of single-child families. According to the National Center for Health Statistics, the number of women

Ann Garcelon, "One Can Be Wonderful," *Redbook*, March 1988. Reprinted with permission.

between the ages of 30 and 34 who have only one child rose from 11.8 percent in 1966, to 22.1 percent in 1985. The fact that these women are in their thirties suggests that these women will not have more children. Given that more women are working outside the home, that birth-control methods are now more reliable, that women are marrying later and that child-rearing costs continue to rise, the number of single-child families in the U.S. is likely to grow in coming years.

As the number of single-child families continues to increase, researchers and psychiatrists have begun turning their attention to the only child—and have come up with some unexpected findings. A number of recent studies have resulted in evidence that verifies what many parents have suspected all along—that only children can turn out just as well as those with siblings. In fact, these studies suggest that they may actually do somewhat better than children with siblings in terms of overall adjustment and accomplishments in later life.

"The time for the one-child family has come," says Hawke, who conducted her own study of 105 such children ranging in age from eight to 66 years, the results of which were later published in a book she coauthored entitled, *One Child by Choice* (Prentice Hall, 1977). Hawke's findings have since been corroborated by Toni Falbo, Ph.D., a professor in the Department of Educational Psychology, University of Texas at Austin, and a leader in research on onlys. Dr. Falbo compiled the results of a number of studies, including her own, in her book, *The Single-Child Family* (Guilford Press, 1984), and concluded that there is little evidence to support the old stereotypes.

"These children are not maladjusted, lonely or selfish," says Dr. Falbo. "They perform well on intelligence and achievement tests and do not differ consistently from other children in their levels of self-esteem and general mental health."

Perhaps the most persistent—and onerous—belief about onlys is that they are spoiled. But, according to Falbo, "Only children are not more selfish by nature than any other children. In fact, children who are born last in a family tend to show more signs of being spoiled than do onlys." Other research findings include:

• Only children do not show signs of being less stable or more neurotic than children with siblings.

• Reports from adult-aged onlys indicate that they are as happy or happier than adults with siblings in terms of their career choices, lifestyles, health and hobbies.

• Only children have *not* been found to be significantly lonelier than others. They have fewer friends in general, but have as many close friendships as do children with siblings.

• Only children are more likely to take responsibility for their own lives instead of blaming their families or other people for their mistakes or problems.

"Only children are not more selfish by nature."

• Only children from two-parent families outscored two-parent children with one sibling on 25 of 32 tests given in such areas as math and reading comprehension.

• Only children demonstrate superior verbal skills, which may develop because they receive more attention from their parents and other adults. This increased interaction with adults may explain why they also perform so well on language-based intelligence tests.

• Only children are generally high achievers and gain more prestige in their work than others do.

• Only children have higher educational aspirations, perform better academically and complete slightly more years of formal education than do children with siblings.

• Only children do not have higher divorce rates.

• Only children tend to express a higher degree of maturity and social sensitivity at an earlier age than their peers do.

Do Only Children "Have It All"?

Most adult onlys acknowledge that there are definite advantages to their only-child status. Eighty-six percent of the group Sharryl Hawke studied said that these advantages include "avoiding sibling rivalry, more parental attention and enjoying greater affluence."

This "greater affluence" is experienced in all areas of their lives: They are the sole recipients of their parents' love, attention *and* financial resources, which can mean anything from being given their own TV set to being guaranteed a better college education. And as one only child put it, "You get all the presents."

Says Robert Westfall, age 39, an only child and builder from East Hampton, New York, "There are two things I couldn't have that I wanted. One was a monkey. The other was a black leather jacket."

Of course, the most important resource parents can offer a child is love, and since the only child is never dethroned by a later sibling, he or she remains the prince or princess of the family for life. According to Lucille K. Forer, Ph.D., a clinical psychologist in private practice in Malibu, California, and author of *The Birth Order Factor* (Pocket Books, 1976), this can be a double-edged sword. Says Forer, "The first child receives the full force of a parent's love, standards, attitudes and values. But the only child also receives the full force of a parent's disciplinary style and protectiveness."

In feeling the "full force" of a parent's love, a special closeness often develops between onlys and their parents which is unparalleled among children with siblings. In families with more than one child, compounded pressures and responsibilities generally don't allow for the same kind of intense parent/child relationship to develop. Says Hawke, "Only children often feel very secure because of the undivided attention and support they receive from their parents and the intimate sharing that takes place between them."

Says Mary Ruth Caldwell, 41, an only child and interior designer in Birmingham, Alabama, who is now raising two children of her own, "I loved the attention I got from my parents and grandparents. They always had time for me. I realize that I was 'it' for my parents. And now my children are 'it' for me."

Only—But Not Lonely

Although some onlys do say they envied other children the companionship of siblings, studies indicate that, on the whole, they do not report having felt lonelier than those with siblings. Some younger only children, however, reported having a close pet or making up imaginary friends for companionship. Says Hawke, "Although studies show that as many as thirty percent of all children have imaginary companions at some time, onlys seem more prone to such fantasies, perhaps because they spend more time by themselves or because their imaginations are more stimulated by the books and experiences that are showered upon them."

Indeed, some onlys said they were accustomed to spending time alone, and attributed much of their creative success to their ability to do so constructively. One such only child is screenwriter Richard Tuggle, 39, who remembers many happy summers spent on the beach with his dog. "I don't recall ever feeling lonely," says Tuggle. "Being alone did make me use my imagination more than my personality. And I think it also helped me to be more independent."

Robert Westfall also feels that time spent alone as an only child "helps you to know yourself better at a younger age."

Only-child Jack Topchik, a journalist from East Windsor, New Jersey, says that he does remember feeling very lonely—especially in the evenings after dinner. But in spite of his loneliness, he points out that it hasn't stopped him from enjoying an "extremely happy marriage" of 19 years and a close relationship with his two sons.

"Only children have not been found to be significantly lonelier than others."

Dr. Falbo's studies also found that an only's time spent alone—or with adult company—can be a definite plus. Says Falbo: "Only children tend to choose more solitary hobbies such as stamp collecting and they read more than other children do. But our research also shows that onlys are more achievement-oriented than children with siblings. In a sense, the amount of time spent alone in childhood can actually be an asset rather than a drawback for them." But it's not clear to what degree the child's drive to succeed stems from parental pressure and how much originates within the child. Falbo's research indicates, however, that "in the main, the vast majority of onlys have parents who have high, but not unrealistic, expectations of them. Because the pressure to succeed is generally not disproportionate to the child's own goals, abilities and interests, the child is better able to go on to succeed as an adult."

Too Much of a Good Thing?

While onlys clearly enjoy advantages that children with siblings can only dream about, these advantages *can* be a liability if parents do not balance their love and generosity with an awareness of the importance of not "overdoing it." "Being an only child presents problems just as any position in the birth order does," says Hawke. "But the problems of the only child are different, not necessarily worse."

One area of concern for almost all parents is whether they are spoiling their child. In her study of onlys, Hawke found that few felt they had been spoiled or were more selfish in later life because they had had more possessions than other children.

"I wasn't spoiled because I was so strictly disciplined," says only-child Rita Robins, a nurse from Memphis, Tennessee, who defines "spoiled" as having every desire satisfied on demand. "When I went visiting with my mother as a little girl, I had to sit with both feet on the floor and my hands folded in my lap for up to three hours sometimes. I couldn't get up unless I had to go to the bathroom. And my mother didn't want me to be selfish, so she insisted

that I share my toys with neighborhood children and learn to give of my time and myself in other ways."

Those only children in Hawke's study who said that they had been spoiled felt that this had happened not because of the possessions they had received, but because they had sensed that their parents were trying to buy their love. Clearly, a parent's motives and attitude in meeting a child's needs and desires is a key factor in whether a child becomes spoiled.

Parents of only children must also be careful not to compete with each other for their child's love, or let the child become an overly important member of the family. "The child will be quick to perceive the excessive dedication of one or both parents," says Murray Kappelman, M.D., professor of pediatrics and Director of the Division of Behavioral and Developmental Pediatrics at the University of Maryland School of Medicine in Baltimore. Dr. Kappelman also feels that parents should be careful not to "give all" to their only child. Limits on possessions and privileges should be set, he says, and priorities must be established within the family as a whole in order to keep the desires of the child in balance with the needs of the parents. . . .

Clearly only children are presented with a unique set of challenges *and* rewards. But when parents are careful to provide them with the right combination of love and discipline, onlys are just as likely as children from larger families to grow into productive, loving and emotionally stable adults.

Ann Garcelon is a free-lance writer in East Hampton, New York.

"Mothering takes sacrifice. For the first few months, it's an around-the-clock, physical job for which you'll get little praise."

viewpoint **3**

Parenting Should Be a Full-Time Job

Sheila Graham

In 1981, I wrote an article on the child-care crisis in the Western world. Looking back over those years, it's amazing how much the situation has changed.

No, the crisis hasn't gone away. It is worse—and potentially much worse. The change is in the way people view the problem. What I described as "emergency tactics" even until the late 1970s—mother going to work—is now considered by many as the status quo.

Today in the United States, 54 percent of married women with children under age 6 work outside the home and the figure is growing. Compare that with 6 percent in 1956.

That particular statistic especially interested me because 1956 was the year my first child was born. Those were the days before natural childbirth, and father in the delivery room, or mother at work in the office, were the popular trends.

My Obsession

Somehow or other, along with my first child came a personal concern for her so overwhelming that I was amazed. I couldn't see enough of her. I couldn't do enough for her.

Seeing those big blue eyes (they turned brown later), framed by long dark lashes, looking up at me so intently from that chubby apple-round face, I knew my life had changed forever.

I determined to breast-feed so that the nurses would have to bring her to me from the nursery every few hours. None of the mothers I knew breast-fed their babies, but I didn't care.

My poor mother, who came to help us in those first few weeks, had to live with my obsession after we returned home from the hospital. She was a good sport, carefully disinfecting her hands with alcohol each time before touching "my baby."

I'm afraid I was almost as intense with our other children, although, in time, I did relax enough to learn to appreciate my mother's help much more.

Remembering those strong, nurturing feelings, when I see the rising statistics of mothers in the work force, leaving their infants in someone else's care, many times in questionable surroundings with equally questionable caretakers, my heart goes out to them.

With the lack of proper facilities and competent caretakers, and the fear of child abuse, no wonder so many mothers feel guilty and frustrated.

Missing the Point?

But why do we have this problem? Are we missing the point somewhere here? Is the child-care problem in the United States and other Western nations a lack of enough day-care facilities and qualified personnel, or is it that mothers are going back to work much too soon after their children are born?

Let's examine the question further. . . .

Human infants acquire more knowledge before they are a year old than they will in any other comparable year of their lives. Before babies can reach out, some researchers find that they have stored up, through sight, information about an object, and are not totally surprised at its shape when able to handle it.

A baby quickly learns to recognize mother and definitely prefers her face and voice. (And more and more researchers are emphasizing the importance of the father in a child's beginning years of life, as well as later.)

Stunted Development

By the time the baby is 5 or 6 months old, most mental and physical abilities acquired will depend upon the response and interest of parents, especially the mother.

A baby left alone for long periods becomes not only lonely, but also frustrated. He or she is not able to exercise, and thus develop, all the new skills he or she is learning. Later the frequency with which the infant expresses himself in making sounds will decrease and the child's language development will slow.

More and more experts are acknowledging that infants and toddlers do not thrive physically, mentally and emotionally in day-care institutions.

The Development of Love

Even more sobering, studies are revealing that a child's ability to form a lasting attachment to another human being—his capacity to love—is learned before age 3. And that this ability to form a lasting mutual attachment is inexorably tied in with the formulation of the child's conscience. In other words, no human attachment equals no proper sense of conscience.

From studies over the last 20 to 30 years infant psychologist Selma Fraiberg states: "We have learned that the human qualities of enduring love and commitment to love are forged during the first two years of life. On this point there is a consensus among scientists from a wide range of disciplines.

"We are living in times," Professor Fraiberg continues, "when there are voices which denigrate the human family and even cry for its dissolution or its recomposition. I cannot identify the voices of infant psychologists among them" (*Every Child's Birthright: In Defense of Mothering*).

It's unnerving to visualize what final effect the emotional near abandonment of our children will have upon our society.

A Valuable Occupation

Too long has women's value as the primary nurturers and educators of their children been downgraded. Women who choose to stay home with their children should never again feel they have to apologize for their occupation.

My question to those considering day care from almost day one is, should you consider having children? If your career is at such a critical stage that you can't make the sacrifice of a few years to give the care every human being needs for emotional stability, perhaps you shouldn't bring children into the world at this time.

At some point or other, careers can be interrupted, with little or no repercussions. The nurturing and care of your most personal precious product, your infant child, cannot.

Of course, mothering takes sacrifice. For the first few months, it's an around-the-clock, physical job for which you'll get little praise. But what rewards!

The intense nurturing of another human being defined as mothering builds a relationship like no other. You can experience this kind of deep,

interpersonal closeness in no other way. Do you want to miss that?

Broken homes are a tragedy. Children need two loving, concerned parents (especially their mothers, at an early age) to help them develop into mature adults capable of loving and caring for other human beings. Adults who can enrich the lives of others with their own unique creativity, who have exercised their God-given right, guided by loving parents, of independent thought and action—parents are responsible for developing such character in their young children.

"Children need two loving, concerned parents."

Preserving the nuclear family is not the panacea for all the world's social ills. In the Western world, especially in America's mobile society, children have been robbed of the stable, extended family ties enjoyed by their grandparents.

Many young people have little sense of the past and less regard for the wisdom of their elders. It should come as no surprise that youths have been wandering around for the last three decades wondering who they are.

Without the support of the extended family, parents' responsibilities today have never been more important. Child rearing is doubly difficult.

Children need both their parents more than ever. To avoid future deep-set emotional problems, there is no substitute for mothers during those early years.

Sheila Graham is associate editor of The Plain Truth.

viewpoint 4

Parenting Should Not Be a Full-Time Job

Barbara Ehrenreich

I was saddened to read that a group of young women is planning a conference on that ancient question: Is it possible to raise children and have a career at the same time? A group of young *men*—now that would be interesting. But I had thought that among women the issue had been put to rest long ago with the simple retort: Is it possible to raise children, *without* having some dependable source of income with which to buy them food, clothing, and Nintendo?

Of course, what the young women are worried about is whether it's possible to raise children *well* while at the same time maintaining one's membership in the labor force. They have heard of "quality time." They are anxious about "missing a stage." They are afraid they won't have the time to nudge their offsprings' tiny intellects in the direction of the inevitable SATs.

And no wonder they are worried: while everything else in our lives has gotten simpler, speedier, more microwavable and user-friendly, child-raising seems to have expanded to fill the time no longer available for it. At least this is true in the trendsetting, post-yuppie class, where it is not uncommon to find busy young lawyers breast-feeding until the arrival of molars, reserving entire weekdays for the company of five-year-olds, and feeling guilty about not ironing the diapers.

In Your Spare Time

This is not only silly but dangerous. Except under the most adverse circumstances—such as homelessness, unsafe living conditions, or lack of spouse and child care—child-raising was not *meant* to be a full-time activity. No culture on earth outside of mid-century suburban America has ever deployed one woman per child without simultaneously assigning her such

major productive activities as weaving, farming, gathering, temple maintenance, and tent building. The reason is that full-time, one-on-one child-raising is not good for women *or* children. And it is on the strength of that anthropological generalization, as well as my own two decades of motherhood, that I offer you my collected tips on *how to raise children at home in your spare time.*

1. Forget the "stages." The women who are afraid to leave home because they might "miss a stage" do not realize that all "stages" last more than 10 minutes. Sadly, some of them last 15 years or more. Even the most cursory parent, who drops in only to change clothes and get the messages off the answering machine, is unlikely to miss a "stage." Once a "stage" is over—and let us assume it is a particularly charming one, involving high-pitched squeals of glee and a rich flow of spittle down the chin—the best thing you can do is *forget it* at once. The reason for this is that no self-respecting six-year-old wants to be reminded that she was once a fat little fool in a high chair; just as no 13-year-old wants to be reminded that she was ever, even for a moment, a six-year-old.

I cannot emphasize this point strongly enough: the parent who insists on remembering the "stages"—and worse still, bringing them up—risks turning that drool-faced little darling into a *life-long enemy.* I mean, try to see it from the child's point of view: suppose you were condemned to being two and a half feet tall, unemployed and incontinent for an indefinite period of time. Would you want people reminding you of this unfortunate phase for the rest of your life?

2. Forget "quality time." I tried it once on May 15, 1978. I know because it is still penciled into my 1978 appointment book. "Kids," I announced, "I have 45 minutes. Let's have some quality time!" They looked at me dully in the manner of rural retirees confronting a visitor from the Census

Bureau. Finally one of them said, in a soothing tone, "Sure, Mom, but could it be after *Gilligan's Island?*"

Secrets of Communicating

The same thing applies to "talks," as in "Let's sit down and have a little talk." In response to that— or the equally lame "How's school?"—any self-respecting child will assume the demeanor of a prisoner of war facing interrogation. The only thing that works is *low-quality* time: time in which you— and they—are ostensibly doing something else, like housework. Even a two-year-old can dust or tidy and thereby gain an exaggerated sense of self-importance. In fact, this is the only sensible function of housework; the other being to create the erroneous impression that you do not live with children after all.

Also, do not underestimate the telephone as a means of parent-child communication. Teenagers especially recognize it as an instrument demanding full disclosure, in infinite detail, of their thoughts, ambitions, and philosophical outlook. If you want to know what's on their minds, call them from work. When you get home, they'll be calling someone else.

3. Do not overload their intellects. Many parents, mindful of approaching nursery school entrance exams, PSATs, GREs, and so forth, stay up late into the night reading back issues of *Scientific American* and the *Cliff's Notes* for the *Encyclopaedia Britannica*. This is in case the child should ask a question, such as "why do horses walk on their hands?" The *overprepared* parent answers with a 20-minute disquisition on evolution, animal husbandry, and DNA, during which the child slinks away in despair, determined never to ask a question again, except possibly the indispensable "Are we there yet?"

The part-time parent knows better, and responds only in vague and elusive ways, letting her voice trail off and her eyes wander to some mythical landscape, as in: "Well, they don't when they fight. . . . No, then they rear up. . . . Or when they fly . . . like Pegasus . . . mmmm." This system invariably elicits a stream of eager questions, which can then be referred to a more reliable source.

A Stunted Adult

4. Do not attempt to mold them. First, because it takes too much time. Second, because a child is not a salmon mousse. A child is a temporarily disabled and stunted version of a larger person, whom you will someday know. Your job is to help them overcome the disabilities associated with their size and inexperience so that they get on with being that larger person, and in a form that you might *like* to know.

Hence the part-time parent encourages self-reliance in all things. For example, from the moment my children mastered Pidgin English, they were taught one simple rule: never wake a sleeping adult. I was

mysterious about the consequences, but they became adept, at age two, at getting their own cereal and hanging out until a reasonable hour. Also, contrary to widespread American myth, no self-respecting toddler enjoys having wet and clammy buns. Nor is the potty concept alien to the one-year-old mind. So do not make the common mistake of withholding the toilet facilities until the crisis of nursery school matriculation forces the issue.

5. Do not be afraid they will turn on you, someday, for being a lousy parent. They *will* turn on you. They will also turn on the full-time parents, the cookie-making parents, the Little League parents, and the all-sacrificing parents. If you are at work every day when they get home from school, they will turn on you, eventually, for being a selfish, neglectful careerist. If you are home every day, eagerly awaiting their return, they will turn on you for being a useless, unproductive layabout. This is all part of the normal process of "individuation," in which one adult ego must be trampled into the dust in order for one fully formed teenage ego to emerge. Accept it.

Not a Profession

Besides, a part-time parent is unlikely to ever harbor that most poisonous of all parental thoughts: "What I gave up for you . . . !" No child should have to take the rap for wrecking a grown woman's brilliant career. The good part-time parent convinces her children that they are positive assets, without whose wit and insights she would never have gotten the last two promotions.

"A part-time parent is unlikely to ever harbor that most poisonous of all parental thoughts: 'What I gave up for you . . . !'"

---

6. Whether you work outside the home or not, never tell them that being a mommy is your "job." Being a mommy is a relationship, not a profession. Nothing could be worse for a child's self-esteem than to think that you think that being with her is *work*. She may come to think that you are involved in some obscure manufacturing process in which she is only the raw material. She may even come to think that her real mom was switched at birth, and that you are the baby-sitter. Which leads to my final tip:

*7. Even if you are not a part-time parent, even if you haven't the slightest intention of entering the wide world of wage earning, *pretend you are one.**

Barbara Ehrenreich is contributing editor to Ms., a monthly feminist magazine.

Government Policies Can Help the Family

Nancy Folbre

Families invoke certain ideals of reciprocity and commitment. They are supposed to function as a miniature socialist society—from each according to his or her ability, to each according to his or her need. To some extent, families realize these ideals. Think, for a minute, of the sum total of resources devoted to caring for the helpless and dependent—children, the elderly, the sick, the handicapped. Although we haven't managed to measure such effort and expenditure with much accuracy, we know that most of it takes place in families. . . .

What's wrong with the family? Nothing's wrong with the family per se, but several things are wrong with patriarchal families. Among them, lack of equality—the family as, literally, the family of man. Women have fewer rights and more responsibilities than men, and are subject to domination and exploitation in the home as well as outside it. Second, lack of freedom—women often lack the viable alternatives that would allow them to freely choose and actively shape family life, while the state constrains both men and women by defining marriage in strictly heterosexual terms and permitting discrimination on the basis of sexual preference. Finally, the patriarchal family suffers from lack of commitment—despite their economic advantages, men often default on their parental responsibilities, leaving women to raise children on their own.

Notice that the first two censures are very much in keeping with the liberal democratic tradition, quarreling with restrictions on individual freedom and opportunity. But the third censure is somewhat different, because it suggests that men may have too much freedom (rather than women having too little) where children are concerned. But as one (non-socialist) feminist commented: "Defenders of the family seem to think that we have already gone too far, that the problem of this painful and confusing time is too much freedom. I think there is no such thing as too much freedom, only too little nerve." To my mind, here's where socialism comes in, moving beyond the discourse of rights to the discourse of obligation.

Women's Gains and Losses

Rights and obligations are often at odds, and socialists have something to learn from the way the tension between the two has hampered feminist activism. Women have made some important gains in recent years in the areas of equality and freedom. But women, particularly mothers, have suffered serious losses in the area of family commitments. In *The Hearts of Men*, Barbara Ehrenreich tells a convincing story about the way men have welcomed those changes in women's rights that have reduced men's obligations to help provide for their children. In *The Divorce Revolution*, Lenore Weitzman documents the ways that no-fault divorce laws have forced women to pay a very high price for personal independence.

Many studies, including Ruth Sidel's *Women and Children Last*, show how increases in the percentage of families maintained by women alone have increased the incidence of poverty among women and children. Rising illegitimacy rates, poor enforcement of child support responsibilities and declining levels of public assistance all suggest that the costs of raising children (never equally shared) are increasingly being shifted to women.

Many individual men have benefited from women's increased contribution of market income. But if time-budget studies are any indication, men have done little to compensate for increases in the length of women's work days. And contrary to the *Three Men and a Baby* stereotype, men don't seem to

Nancy Folbre, "Whither Families?" *Socialist Review*, October-December 1988. Reprinted with permission.

be spending more time taking care of the kids. Studies to date show that when couples have children, men's leisure time remains largely unchanged, while women's leisure time (including, but not limited to sleep) virtually disappears.

The New Right, of course, argues cause and effect: feminism has "destabilized" the family. Phyllis Schlafly constantly reiterated this point in her tireless efforts to squelch the Equal Rights Amendment. Most feminists, on the other hand, see men's defection as a manifestation of a form of continuing male power—feminism hasn't gone far enough. In particular, women have proved unable to fully enforce men's obligations to family and society. . . .

A criticism of the mainstream feminist movement, however, does not correspond to a criticism of feminism. Nor can the tenor of the mainstream feminist movement of the 1970s and early 1980s be reduced to class differences or professional "selfishness." Voices were raised early on about the importance of women's family work and the need for public support for childrearing. But those voices did not harmonize with liberal democratic discourse. And the demands they articulated sounded less sexy and more expensive than equal rights. As a result, they were largely drowned out.

"Voices were raised early on about the importance of women's family work and the need for public support for childrearing."

The New Right chorus, which swelled in the 1980s, was also far from unanimous. Some voices expressed only shrill opposition to equality of opportunity and reproductive rights. But others simply swore allegiance to the flag of family commitment. This subtext could almost be described as "socialism in one family"—a conservative version of the old "small is beautiful" argument, or sharing on a small scale. This argument is perfectly consistent with opposition to public assistance—large institutions such as the state can never really solve social problems, only worsen them by weakening families.

Crucial to this argument is an idealization of women that is ironically reminiscent of the traditional Marxian idealization of the proletariat. Women's interests become society's interests, not because women are a "universal class," but because they willingly subordinate their own interests to others. George Gilder, in particular, extols women's special capacity for altruism. Women's love domesticates men, channels their aggressive instincts into healthy breadwinning activities.

It sounds like a threat (and perhaps it is intended as one)—if women don't take responsibility for children and the family, nobody will. . . .

Unlike mainstream feminism, the New Right offers a theory of social obligation—but the theory is little more than a presumption of innate, God-given family love that persists until and unless it is interfered with by the state. And while the New Right believes that individual rights should hold sway in the marketplace, it denies them any place within the home. The misplaced insights of conservative social thought should be an impetus to the development of a new feminism—a bold assertion of both rights *and* obligations.

The New Feminism

I am not suggesting that feminism should slacken its concern with equal rights. Rather, feminists need to think about what family members owe each other *and* what society owes families. Also, moving beyond the ethical realm of obligation, feminists need to explain how and why the weakening of the traditional patriarchal family has had both positive and negative effects on women and children. And, finally, feminists need to offer a strategy for strengthening and supporting the positive aspects of family life, a strategy that should include detailed reforms in federal, state, and local policy.

Right now, it seems as though the last is starting first. Activists, as usual, move faster than theoreticians. Coming from the civil rights, rather than the feminist tradition, Marian Wright Edelman has steered the Children's Defense Fund firmly towards advocacy of progressive social programs that would target needy families and their children. Representative Pat Schroeder is also committed to building a political constituency based on progressive family issues. The themes she raised on her "Great American Family Tour" are broad based: lack of health insurance coverage, lack of job-protected parental leave, lack of affordable day care and housing, and the need for pay equity policies.

As they now stand, these political initiatives are limited, pragmatic, almost defensive responses to the New Right. Pat Schroeder almost sounds convincing when she explains that families have changed, that most politicians are simply out of touch with the current realities of US family life. But more than forgetfulness or mere oversight is involved. And more than Marian Wright Edelman's famous moral tenacity will be required to make change.

Neither Schroeder nor Edelman take much trouble to explain what they mean by families, leaving implicit the conventional biological/legal definition. As a result, "chosen families," gay and lesbian couples, as well as many individuals, are implicitly excluded. Finally, both seem to accede to the most convenient explanation of the weakening of families—the strains imposed by women's increased labor market participation. Even when accompanied by the insistence that most women *must* work in order to help provide for their families, this explanation leaves men out of the picture. It politely ignores the fact that men's behavior—particularly their disinclination to take economic responsibility for children either in the family or in the polity— accounts for many of the family's problems.

A progressive family policy cannot be based upon any idealization of the traditional patriarchal family— the family as it was *before* women entered the labor force, or the family as it *would be* if male unemployment rates were not so high. A progressive family policy must grow out of a bold, open discussion of the contradictory character of the patriarchal family—a critique of its maldistribution of rights and obligations tempered by some appreciation of the way it enforced certain family obligations and rewarded certain types of family labor. . . .

A New Family Policy

If we appreciate the contradictory character of the family, we can reaffirm our allegiance to its ideals of reciprocity and commitment. But not without substantial effort to redefine its rights and obligations. My reading of the history of "family default" of youth in general and men in particular persuades me that family life cannot rely on purely personal commitment, but requires agreement to formal and enforceable obligations. A progressive family policy requires progressive family law reform.

The traditional definition of a family is based on biological kinship and legal contracts such as adoption and marriage. As US law now stands, this definition is arbitrary. The US government currently prohibits homosexual marriage, denying such partners eligibility for family related benefits, such as Social Security, that are not insubstantial. Marriage, divorce, and paternity laws in most states still embody serious inequities.

Family law should be modified to ensure fairness and to allow individuals more freedom and flexibility in formalizing their commitments to each other. But these commitments should be explicit. Otherwise, children, the elderly, the sick, the disabled and the women who often take care of them will be at risk. For the same reasons, family law should recognize the importance of family labor and ensure that those who specialize in unpaid labor are not penalized when formal commitments are ignored or dissolved.

One specific and controversial example is the issue of child support. Growing awareness of inadequate levels of child support and poor enforcement of court-awarded child support payments have led to stricter enforcement policies on both the national and state level. Many progressive activists have criticized this emphasis on strict enforcement, arguing that it is punitive, inadequate, and misplaced. Existing legislation does indeed have a

punitive component—mothers who will not reveal their children's paternity face partial or total loss of AFDC [Aid to Families with Dependent Children] benefits.

Recognizing Social Obligations

But some form of child support enforcement is necessary. Fathers share an obligation with mothers to provide for their children—poverty and unemployment seem like pretty lame excuses when mothers suffer equally, if not more, from the same problems. Nor does family obligation necessarily weaken the case for social obligation—in either case, individuals who take a free ride on the efforts of others diminish cooperative energy and undermine collective effort.

Through Social Security and Medicare, the US formally recognizes a certain social obligation to provide for the health and well-being of the elderly. In the years since 1935 coverage has been extended and poverty among the elderly has been reduced— although it still remains far too high. The point here is that the elderly receive entitlements, while mothers and children in poverty can only ask for welfare. But families who are raising children are performing socially necessary, important work and they are entitled to public assistance.

Current US policy includes an implicit entitlement— the child and childcare deductions in federal income taxes. But this current policy (like the expanded tax breaks some pro-family groups advocate) primarily benefits the well-to-do. A family allowance program, similar to those common in Western European countries, would provide a substitute both for tax subsidies and for AFDC, particularly if supplemented by job training and childcare programs. All families with children under 18 would be eligible regardless of their marital status, whereas current AFDC assistance is limited in most states to families maintained by women alone.

"A progressive family policy cannot be based upon any idealization of the traditional patriarchal family."

Non-parents, as well as those who have already raised their children, might object to this social claim on their income. But the Social Security system has already given them a stake in the future earnings of the younger generation, which will be used to finance their retirement. In fact, the current system actually redistributes income *from* individuals who devote time and energy to raising children (which provides no claim to Social Security income) to individuals who specialize in earning a high-wage income (and therefore higher payments at retirement). For married couples, these two may balance out, but the increasing frequency of divorce means that single mothers who do a large share of the work of raising the next generation can expect little retirement income in old age.

Growing Economic Difficulties

The work of childrearing deserves respect as well as remuneration. Many small-minded and mean-spirited proponents of punitive workfare programs are unwilling to concede either of these. But a cross-class, cross-race constituency of parents, mothers in particular, recognizes the growing economic difficulties of raising children and would like to counter them with a whole range of new entitlements.

The successful implementation of a family allowance system hinges on development of other, related programs. In the absence of job training programs, job opportunities, and good childcare facilities, family allowances could increase women's tendency to specialize in child care and isolate them in the home. It could also increase the birth rate. But even where family allowances have been introduced with explicitly pro-natalist motives, fertility rates have continued to decline. The biggest difference between the US and Western European families is that the incidence of poverty among women with young children is far lower there.

"Family life cannot rely on purely personal commitment, but requires agreement to formal and enforceable obligations."

At least two other specific policies should supplement a family allowance system. In modest form, both are currently on the congressional agenda—guaranteed family leave from work and more resources for high quality, affordable child care. In the US today, less than 40 percent of all women workers are covered by any contractual provisions for pregnancy leave, very few men have a paternity leave option, and many workers forced to take time off to cope with family illness lose their jobs. House Bill 925, sponsored by Representative Pat Schroeder, would require employers to provide workers with 10 weeks of family leave to care for a newborn, newly-adopted child or to care for a seriously ill child or parent, and 15 weeks of medical leave to care for themselves when they are seriously ill. . . .

It's important to invoke the social family, to openly contest the conservative claim that private families can or should solve social problems. And therefore to combine pro-family policies with a larger assertion of public and community responsibility. We need major improvements in health, education, housing,

job training and a guaranteed right to a job. We are all entitled and obligated to life in a fully democratic economy.

Nancy Folbre is an associate professor of economics at the University of Massachusetts at Amherst.

Government Policies Hurt the Family

Robert W. Lee

Revolutionaries and collectivists regard the institution of the family as a rival to the state. Conservatives see it otherwise. The federal Working Group on the Family was established by the Reagan Administration in February of 1986 to study how government at all levels could be made less hostile to American families. Its report, released in December of the same year, correctly observed that "every totalitarian movement of the 20th century has tried to destroy the family. . . . The essence of modern totalitarianism has been to substitute the power of the State for the rights, responsibilities, and authority of the family" as well as the individual. The Working Group on the Family . . . found that, "[w]here there are strong families, the freedom of the individual expands and the reach of the State contracts. Where family life weakens and fails, government advances, intrudes, and ultimately compels."

The Working Group on the Family also noted the extent to which freedom of enterprise and sound American families are linked. While some "contend that the consumer ethic of capitalism undermined family values," it is "more true that neither the modern family nor the free-enterprise system would long survive without the other." The report quotes Dr. Allan C. Carlson, president of the Rockford Institute, to the effect that free enterprise—through "its devotion to human freedom, its creation of wealth, and its demand for personal responsibility—made the modern family possible. And the modern family—by its channeling of the unleashed individual toward natural and necessary social tasks, by its mobility, by its unique motivational psychology, and by its linkage to an inherited moral code—made the free-enterprise system possible."

Robert W. Lee, "How Government Has Made War Against the American Family," *Conservative Digest*, February 1988. Reprinted with permission.

The family is our society's most basic social institution. It is the child's first and most important school, providing a wealth of knowledge and information before he or she ever enters a classroom. And no economic institution has ever surpassed the family for supporting the vulnerable young and old. The family provides food, clothing, shelter, and recreation for its members, and applies sanctions for infractions of rules and values which govern the home. By its nature and assignment, the family is competitive with civil government in many ways, and the masters of big government therefore have a powerful incentive to usurp the household's functions in a way that undermines the family.

Government Meets Resistance

If millions of stable families are permitted to impart their own unique traditions and outlook to succeeding generations, the resulting variety in attitudes about everything from religion to styles of clothing and politics makes it difficult for bureaucrats and social planners to impose their own standards without meeting serious resistance. Such resistance can be reduced, however, if parental authority is undermined, "generation gaps" are encouraged, hostility between the sexes is cultivated and divorce made as easy as marriage; if family wealth is stripped away by government-spawned inflation, and transferred to the state by heavy income and estate taxation; if women are pressured and indoctrinated to abandon their maternal responsibilities and work outside the home just to make ends meet; if warehouses for the elderly can be made socially acceptable; *etc.* The goal of collectivists is to make everyone dependent on (and loyal to) the state rather than to so highly individualistic, eccentric, and competitive an institution as the traditional family.

In a section devoted to taxes, the report the Working Group on the Family reminds us that, especially during the 1960s and 1970s, "the Federal tax code meant bad news for the American family. It sent a message to every household in the land: the traditional family of parents and children was of no importance to policymakers—and tax spenders—in Washington. Nearly every special-interest group managed to protect itself in tax legislation except for the most important part of our economic and social system: husband, wife, and children." For instance, between "1960 and 1984, the average tax rate for a couple with two children climbed 43 percent. For a couple with four kids, the increase was an incredible 223 percent."

A major part of the problem was the refusal of Congress to increase the personal exemption for dependents to keep up with inflation. Set at $600 in 1948, it would have had to be around $5,000 in 1984 just to have kept pace with inflation. Instead, it was only twenty percent of that—a paltry $1,000. The Reagan tax-reform bill increased the exemption to $2,000, which is a significant step in the right direction, but it still falls far short of what is needed to neutralize the government bias against the family.

Another positive aspect of the Reagan tax law is the increased Earned Income Tax Credit which, by offsetting additional Social Security taxes for low-income families, will reduce their tax load while increasing the work incentive.

Undermining the Family

One important aspect of the tax code which Congress refused to modify in a pro-family manner was the child-care tax credit. As now structured, the credit may be claimed by households with two wage earners but is denied to couples who arrange to raise their own children. As the report of the Working Group points out, this "forces more than half the families of America to pay higher taxes solely because one spouse, usually the wife, has chosen not to work outside the home. She may devote long hours to humanitarian work, community projects, and her family. But her higher taxes subsidize child care for her peers who are in the workplace." Since research clearly indicates that "home care for youngsters is vastly preferable to institutional arrangements," then "if public policy will not favor home rearing of America's boys and girls, at least it should not be perceived as tilting the board in favor of care *outside* the home."

Our heavy "progressive" income tax, combined with inheritance and Social Security taxes, and supplemented by the many anti-family provisions of sundry welfare programs, represents another formidable weapon for transferring economic wealth (and the power which wealth entails) from the family to the state. As the Working Group advised: "To help families, the best step government can take is to let them keep more of their hard-earned money."

The increasing migration of women into the workplace has been accompanied by intense lobbying efforts in behalf of government financed day-care facilities for children. According to the Census Bureau, at least 35 percent of women with children under five years of age now work outside the home full time, while another 20 percent work part time. By comparison, in 1960 less than 20 percent of married mothers with children under age six were employed outside the home either full or part time.

"To help families, the best step government can take is to let them keep more of their hard-earned money."

Not only is institutionalized child care enormously expensive, but a growing body of research indicates that it may harm many children. Yet, rather than face the issue squarely, day-care professionals anxious to promote their industry, feminists who consider government day care essential to their socialist "equality" agenda, and parents unwilling to acknowledge that non-maternal day care might be harmful to their children, have downplayed, distorted, or disregarded the mountain of studies which raise serious questions about the long-term impact of institutional day care on the physical and emotional health of the youngsters involved. . . .

Parents owe it to themselves and their children to become fully informed about the many risks involved in institutionalized day care. Congress should (1) either terminate the tax credit for day care or, at the very least, make such a credit available to traditional families, and (2) increase the tax exemption for dependent children to at least $5,000 to reduce the economic pressure which presently forces many mothers to work outside the home who would prefer personally to nurture their children.

The Marriage Bond

Another significant (but seldom noted) way in which traditional families are undermined is by being made to pay for problems largely created by those who opt for "alternative" lifestyles. Medical authorities and health officials now generally recognize that such situations as bastardy, divorce, day care, homosexuality, and singleness entail added health risks which are placing severe strain on the nation's health-care resources. In contrast, marriage and family life foster good health. But traditional families are unable to enjoy the *economic* benefits of superior health because, as noted in the July 1987 issue of *The Family In America*, such benefits "are siphoned off through welfare-state policies and collectivized health care and are used to pay for the group pathologies of those who have deliberately rejected the moral and social restraints of family life."

Writing in *Social Science And Medicine*, Catherine K. Riessman and Naomi Gerstel reported in 1985 that "one of the most consistent observations in health research is that married [people] enjoy better health than those of other marital statuses." Indeed, researchers at Case Western Reserve University found that even when a marriage is strained it provides a certain amount of protection against serious physical illnesses. They reported that couples who had filed for divorce, but changed their minds, were "less likely than the divorced to be sick enough to be in bed." And the prestigious British medical journal *The Lancet* for August 10, 1985, reported that even marriages between the mentally ill (something long discouraged) are "stable and may even show improved function. . . . The support provided by a shared mental disability may have a beneficial effect."

Singles Plagued with Disease

Certainly single-parent homes (whether a result of divorce or illegitimacy) are plagued with a disproportionate number of illnesses. Dr. James Lynch, professor of psychology at the University of Maryland, reports that divorced and single persons stay in hospitals longer than do married men and women with the same illnesses, and that they also die at much higher rates from cancer and heart disease than do their married counterparts. And the *Journal Of The Royal Society Of Medicine* for October 1982 reported that members of one-parent families also suffer from higher rates of less serious maladies (such as "headaches, backaches, tummy aches, listlessness, depression, [and] a host of other ailments") than do those in two-parent households.

The statistics also show that working women (perhaps due, at least in part, to their greater economic independence) seek divorce more readily than do non-working women, thus placing themselves more at risk for the sundry health problems which accompany divorce. And singles not only stay longer in the hospital, and die more often when suffering from common diseases frequently found among marrieds, but they contract sundry sexually transmitted diseases at a much higher rate than do those who marry. And the situation is worse still for singles who spurn not only marriage but heterosexuality as well, since homosexuals constitute the vast majority of AIDS victims, and also contract gonorrhea, infectious hepatitis A and B, amoebic colon infection, and a number of other exotic diseases at unusually high rates.

Non-marital sexual activity among heterosexuals aggravates health problems in ways other than the mere transmission of disease. For instance, pregnant women who are unmarried are more likely to undergo abortion, and suffer physical and emotional difficulties thereafter, than are married women. When illegitimate babies are not aborted, they usually stay in the hospital both more frequently and for longer periods than do those born within wedlock. And, since a disproportionate number of illegitimate babies are born to teenage mothers, many are premature, and 20 percent of premature babies suffer lifelong birth defects of one type or another.

Family Health Better

Dr. Bryce J. Christensen, editor of *The Family In America*, observes that, given "the disparity between good health of people living in families and the ill health of people living outside of families, a reasonable observer would conclude that government and business officials interested in promoting public health would frame policies that encourage family formation and inhibit family breakup. Instead, at present almost all states permit 'no fault' divorce, while the Federal government enforces a tax policy that in recent decades has favored singles, childless couples, and two-worker households at the expense of traditional families. More egregiously, current insurance and welfare policies force healthy, intact families to pay the medical bills incurred by people who have deliberately avoided family responsibilities and—in many cases—who have repudiated the family as a repressive and outmoded institution."

"Current insurance and welfare policies force healthy, intact families to pay the medical bills incurred by people who have deliberately avoided family responsibilities."

On September 2, 1987, President Reagan responded to these problems and the findings of the Working Group on the Family by issuing an Executive Order which will be an important step toward curbing federal abuse of the family. It requires Executive departments and agencies, when formulating and implementing policies and regulations which significantly impact "family formation, maintenance, and well-being," to assess such measures in light of the following questions:

(1) Does the government action "strengthen or erode the stability of the family and, particularly, the marital commitment?"; (2) does it "strengthen or erode the authority and rights of parents in the education, nurture, and supervision of their children?"; (3) does it "help the family perform its functions, or does it substitute governmental activity for the function?"; (4) does it "increase or decrease family

earnings" and do "the proposed benefits . . . justify the impact on the family budget?"; (5) can it "be carried out by a lower level of government or by the family itself?"; (6) "What message, intended or otherwise," does it "send to the public concerning the status of the family?"; and, (7) "What message does it send to young people concerning the relationship between their behavior, their personal responsibility, and the norms of our society?"

Executive departments and agencies are also directed to "identify proposed regulatory and statutory provisions that may have significant potential negative impact on the family well-being and provide adequate rationale on why such a proposal should be submitted."

Conservatives believe that the President is to be commended for his pro-family efforts. We agree with the President that the fact such an Executive Order is necessary to require the bureaucracy to do what it should have been doing as a matter of course is further confirmation of government's hostility toward the family.

It is time for those who believe in the traditional family to become better informed about what is happening . . .; who is undermining the family (and why); and, how the destructive current policies and trends can be reversed. And then we must start fighting back by becoming organized to the point where our political clout overwhelms the intense anti-family pressure from the other side. There is no more important issue than regaining for the American family the ground it has lost, and restoring it to its proper place within our national life.

Robert W. Lee is a contributing editor for the Conservative Digest *in Washington, DC.*

"Homemaking for the sake of one's children and neighborhood is worthy of a woman's and a man's best efforts."

Two-Career Couples Are Sacrificing Family Life

Sara Wenger Shenk

It was an ordinary weekday evening, but the meal was festive. To commemorate my husband Gerald's completion of a difficult writing project, I had prepared two simple and highly spiced Ethiopian dishes for supper. Our sons were pleased that Dad had met his deadline, and even more delighted to rip off pieces of flat pancake-like *injera* and dip them into the red-hot stew.

While dousing flames in his mouth with great gulps of water, our 6-year-old remarked, "I can't believe it! Just the simplest things at home can be so exciting!" I sank back into my chair for a quiet moment of exultation. Gerald's eyes shone across the table.

Our family likes to celebrate—not with a lot of fanfare—but by deliberately marking and enriching moments in time. It's an art we are cultivating after watching too much time slip through our fingers in a frenetic blur. On any ordinary day, there are far too few hallowed moments, particularly in our homes; too few occasions to savor time-honored stories with our children; too few gestures of old-fashioned hospitality; too few festive activities to send our spirits soaring.

Homemaker Role Maligned

Home, the quintessential source of family and companionship, where intimacy and trust are meant to flourish, has become an afterthought, relegated to the fringes of our days. For many families, over-invested or underpaid, wealthy or impoverished, home is a crash-pallet, hardly a place preserved and cultivated for ministry; a battleground, not a thriving hub of simple communal pleasures. The role of "homemaker," for varied reasons, has been maligned almost out of existence.

I think the time has come for a revolution of

priorities at home. Home-based ministry, be it to one's own children, to the neighbors, to the elderly, to those forgotten and left out, needs to be reinvigorated. What better place than the home for children to see Christ-like ministry modeled day after day? What is more needed in our isolationist urban-suburban neighborhoods than homes that provide a warm circle of tender loving care? What could give a greater influx of energy to the church than a growing (rather than shrinking) core of folks free to volunteer for service to the community?

I have entered a veritable mine field—an area of discourse so sensitive and fraught with dilemmas that no matter what is said, someone will feel stepped on. But let me assert that two-parent families that choose to live on one full-time salary or a couple of part-time salaries to free up time for presence at home and voluntary service are making a radical and essential statement about Christian ministry in our day.

I must at least partially qualify what I am suggesting. I know that not everyone has options; very often employment is due to financial or emotional necessity. And surely not every home is made better by having a full-time parent. Many persons (mostly women) who have devoted full time to the home have become disillusioned and bitter. Nor is it always the case that if both parents are employed full time there is no family life or community service. And many single parents manage to hold job and family together with astounding tenacity and valor. Nevertheless, there is good reason to examine further what is at stake in the nurturing of life at home.

There was an article in *The Chicago Tribune* a few years ago about the world's smartest person—a woman with an IQ of 230; a woman so smart that she could chop her IQ in half and still be above average. One remark she made in the newspaper interview was this: "I can't imagine just staying home and doing

Sara Wenger Shenk, "On the Home Front," *Sojourners*, January 1989. Reprinted with permission from *Sojourners*, Box 29272, Washington, DC 20017.

nothing but taking care of someone. Anybody can take care of a baby." This woman also called marriage "stultifying" and said there are too many kids in the world for her to contribute any more. Clearly the implication to be drawn from the above statement is that if you have brains it is beneath your dignity to care for children; and if you stay home and take care of someone, you don't have brains and are doing nothing of value.

Women Are Ambivalent

Opinions about what should happen at home are legion. One young mother commented, "I sometimes wish I had lived 100 years ago when everything wasn't a choice. Then I could have been a traditional mother, spent my days with my kids, and just delighted in them without all this ambivalence about career and identity."

Whether this woman's concept of the reality our foremothers experienced is accurate or not, she put her finger on one of the chief dilemmas contemporary women face: There is now no widespread cultural consensus about who we are as women, wives, and mothers, and what we are supposed to do.

Rare is the woman today who can say, as a woman of my mother's generation said, "I felt no other calling than to get married and to have children." We are called in our generation to a new dimension of freedom and maturity, a new dimension of responsibility for who we become and how we will serve amid an ever-expanding array of options.

One young mother will comment, "Some women aren't as happy staying at home with a child as I am. Nobody should be forced to stay home if it makes them miserable, but I know that I could never leave my baby." Another will complain, "Motherhood is an invisible, low-status occupation with no pay and no time off. Worse yet, a lot of hard work and good intentions can result in failure."

"Rare is the woman today who can say . . . 'I felt no other calling than to get married and to have children.'"

One mother will say, "At least I'm *there* for my kids. You can't just up and make a decision to have kids one day and then expect them to raise themselves. You shouldn't have children unless you can step out of the job market long enough to be with them when they're little." Another will say, "My career is part of who I am. Why should I have to become a different person because I have a baby?" And yet another mother will admit, "I was taught that my career *and* my family should both come first. I was convinced that I could do it all. But I'm exhausted. I simply can't do it all."

Waves of ambivalence swamp the attempts many of us make to be all things to all people. We sometimes regard women who have made different choices than ours with jealousy or antipathy. Many of us harbor an inordinate amount of guilt for failing ourselves, our husbands, or our children. With heightened expectations about what we can become, and also more knowledge about what makes for healthy children, we frequently incriminate ourselves for falling short on one front or another.

Yet despite the painful self-doubts which inevitably accompany times of intense growth, and despite the accusations and jealousies, we are blessed in our day with an enormous flowering of women's gifts. We've discovered on a large scale that women, like men, are good at more things than the traditional roles led us to believe.

Fifty years ago few married women were able to gain employment outside the home. Now 45 percent of the labor force in the United States is women. Fifty years ago only a few medical doctors were women and still fewer were lawyers or engineers. Today 37 percent of the students entering medical schools are women. A third of all students working toward ministerial degrees in the nation's seminaries are now women.

It is frequently acknowledged that women bring complementary and valued qualities to work teams, including a nurturing approach to pastoral care with an inclination to more participatory and less authoritarian approaches to leadership. Women's contributions are needed and welcomed on many, many fronts.

Who Will Care for Children?

But (and here comes the absolutely critical question that begs for an answer), who is willing to care for the children? The Children's Defense Fund and other groups estimate that by 1995 the mothers of two-thirds of all preschoolers will be in the workforce, and some estimates project that 80 percent of mothers of young children will be in the workforce in the 21st century.

Obviously, society will have to gear up for a much more comprehensive day-care program than is now available. Such a move will provide much-needed solutions for many parents who have no choice other than to take their children to others for care.

Widespread day care for very young children, however, results in a radically diminished parental role, meaning increased alienation from an integrated, intimate home life as more and more of a child's life is spent in an institutional world external to a parent's direct control. Are we who have a choice ready to see the parental role at home so radically curtailed?

Again I tread on a mine field. Many child-care situations are pleasant and enrich a child's environment, and mothers and fathers who have enjoyable work often make happier parents than those confined exclusively to child care. I for one am a much more obliging mother because I have work in addition to child care that expands my horizons, and my children in their preschool years enjoyed a pleasant day-care supplement. I am also aware that good day care is far preferable to many debilitating home environments. But the disturbing questions related to the home front continue.

As more and more women leave the home to pursue careers, how are the children affected? Is the flow of mothers toward employment in any way being matched by fathers choosing to remain at home? Is it not actually the case that few men are opting to become primary caregivers, and consequently, on a massive scale, our homes are being drained of parental nurture?

I think it would be accurate to observe that the more choices we have, the less often we, women and men, have chosen for children. It also appears that the more possibilities before us to achieve personal career goals, the more we have come to view children as an obstruction; and that the more we feel able to control our own destiny, the less we are willing to deal with the unpredictable, messy, distracting dynamo that is a child.

How can we know that the children and their parents are not both big losers because of the shrinking amount of time they spend together? Might it not be the case that as more and more of us opt for institutional solutions for child care, we will reap, in future years, a harvest of bitterness from our little ones grown tall who remember that they were given, at best, only secondary consideration; and a flood of regret from aging parents who didn't slow down enough to cherish companionship with small sons and daughters who suddenly grew up and were gone?

Children Need Models

If the number of children in trouble in our society is a significant indicator, our children need us now more than ever. The statistics reveal problems of epidemic proportions. Depression among adolescents continues to increase. The suicide rate of children in the United States has risen 300 percent in 25 years, reaching as many as 6,000 suicides and about half a million suicide attempts annually.

U.S. teens under age 15 are 15 times more likely to give birth than their peers in any other Western nation. Among teen-agers, drug use remains high, with cocaine use on the rise. The abuse of alcohol among teens is very high, with a reasonable estimate that three million 14- to 17-year-olds are problem drinkers.

The National Coalition on Television Violence reports that the average American child will see more than 800 advertisements promoting war toys in a year; war cartoons on American TV increased from less than two hours per week in 1982 to 27 hours per week in 1985, and the sale of war toys increased 600 percent during the same period. Child abuse and child pornography are on the increase.

The incidence of divorce has more than doubled since 1960, and the number of children newly affected by divorce now exceeds one million annually. Forty percent of black children and 20 percent of all children in the United States live in single-parent families. A 1984 estimate of "latchkey children" put their number at eight million.

"The more possibilities before us to achieve personal career goals, the more we have come to view children as an obstruction."

It is far from easy to grow up in North America. The prevalence of these troubles raises important questions about the character of our society, contends Perry London, a professor in the Harvard University Graduate School of Education. No one has yet counted how many youngsters suffer from these psychosocial ills, but even the most conservative statistics show that millions of children are directly at risk from them; all other children, indirectly.

London notes that if children are being well-socialized elsewhere, the schools need only supplement a process that is well-advanced before schools become involved. People intuitively know, he continues, that the formation of character in children depends on adult models and on some implied consensus about cultural rituals, ideals, and expectations. The models are parents, siblings, members of an extended family, stable neighbors.

Modern American society, however, has lost much of its dependable common rituals and figures of reverence. Nor are models of socially acceptable adult roles available as frequently or in as much variety as in the past. Traditional agents of character education have been weakened by the fluidity and heterogeneity of American society. Anonymity has replaced community.

London argues that because of the ravages of "social disorganization and family collapse," the schools must now play a more active role in developing programs that protect children and nurture growth of personality as well as of intellect. "When impediments to sane growth are epidemic among the youth of a nation," London writes, "as is true of American society today, the issues that plague the lives of young people are more than personal problems. They are not simply signs of the health and welfare of children, but of the character of the society, the quality of the civilization, and, perhaps, the prospects for its future."

A friend who visited us, whose husband is working on a doctorate at a major Ivy League school, remarked that in that university community, if you admit that you are a homemaker, "You count for zero." I'm reminded too of a seminary professor who lamented the injustice perpetrated in families because many wives have been obligated to "forgo personal development" in order to care for the family, thus freeing husbands to pursue personal growth.

Where, oh, where did we get this twisted notion that to stay home with children is to stagnate? Who fabricated the fiction that to make a home counts for nothing? Is it barking into the wind to proclaim that homemaking for the sake of one's children and neighborhood is worthy of a woman's *and* a man's best efforts; and that parenting stimulates unparalleled growth in the parents as well?

A father who has chosen to stay home part time with his children writes, "Watching and helping my children grow is the most overwhelmingly beautiful process of which I have ever been part. My children teach me, play with me, help me grow, and heal me. What a marvel to see their lives unfold before me. What a privilege to participate in this. . . . The worth of our relationship is beyond measure."

Unacknowledged Contributions

A woman psychologist observed, "Mothering takes much time and energy that is not put into a career. One must accept the fact that one loses time and salary. But on the other hand, my baby helped significantly in recovery of the use of the right side of my brain [the intuitive, creative, feeling side] and contributed to my career as a therapist. If I were a teacher, minister, or business person, I suspect this contribution would be no less significant."

I strongly suspect that we have lost a great deal of our humanity and freedom inasmuch as we have come to regard the "male" work role as the normative human activity. One must seriously question whether women are liberated simply by being enabled to function like men in the public realm.

"There are clues to a better humanity in the virtues often associated with women and home."

Not long ago a woman in my home church confessed through her tears, in the open sharing time of the service, that she so wants to be like Mary, just sitting at Jesus' feet, but the never-ending, urgent household and hospitality chores preoccupy her time. If guests are invited, food must be

prepared, the toilet must be cleaned. What does one do to mesh real-life demands with sitting at Jesus' feet?

A wise single mother and grandmother responded. I think we are all Mary *and* Martha, she said. There is no reason you can't sit at Jesus' feet while cooking a meal or while cleaning the toilet. The key is *remembering*—remembering that you are free to pray, listen, and worship anytime, anywhere.

One year put a severe strain on my stock of survival skills. When our second son was close to 6 years old, we birthed a daughter. No falling asleep at the breast for this champion wrestler. She needed to be jogged, and that rather energetically, before she surrendered to slumber—and then sleep seemed just an excuse to waken again.

Would we trade her to a gypsy for a nickle? Only in jest. But day after day she sucked life out of me. And our extended family was an ocean away.

I remember shaking with sobs one day after reading a well-written article. The beauty of the piece pierced me, but more than that, I suddenly realized how eternally long it seemed since I had written a word.

From Arrogance to Tenderness

Can I say it, without sounding melodramatic, that this toughest of years has also been most fulfilling? I am given to murmuring on the ragged edges of many days, but nearly every day there are moments when I swell fit to burst with the joy of being with these little people. They truly have remade me, turning a heart of arrogance into a throbbing heart of tenderness. And they continue to convert me day after day toward simple pleasures amid the hurly-burly. The fun, food, and companionship we share, along with another family in the household right upstairs, is surrounding us with a cloak of security, with rhyme and reason, with anticipation and fulfillment, over and over again.

Reclaiming the home turf means resolving to reintegrate men's and women's work and to interweave home and work into a harmonious pattern. Homemaking means to build community with children and neighbors and to establish worship and celebrative rituals that actively shape family traditions.

Children are not liabilities or a drain on personal growth. Nor is home a backwater of ill repute. In our self-indulgent generation, children are a primary source of conversion. Transforming our isolated, privatized dwellings into home-based communities where life and worship are nurtured is a sacred calling.

Now is not the time for airy-headed romanticism that pines for the olden days of little houses on the prairie. Rather, it is a time for hardheaded realism and gutsy determination to make job decisions and personal sacrifices for the common good—the good of our children, ourselves, and our society. With children who thrive on simple pleasures, our work and our entire society can be renewed. We desperately need a revolution of hope at home!

Leading feminist theologian Rosemary Radford Ruether contends in her book *Sexism and Godtalk* that feminism needs to ask whether instead of making the male sphere the norm and attempting to assimilate women into it, it is not necessary to move in the opposite direction. "Should we not take the creation and sustaining of human life as the center," she asks, "and reintegrate alienated maleness into it?"

Clearly, women are not automatically redeemed by being incorporated into male political power and business, Ruether writes; nor will men be automatically redeemed by learning to nurture infants and keep house. Some have idealized the home, overlooking the violence so often present there. And yet there are clues to a better humanity in the virtues often associated with women and home in Western society if those virtues are not locked within an exclusive female sphere.

Revive Art of Homemaking

The time has come to revive the art of homemaking and to rekindle the hearth; to recapture the trembling wonder of a child that shatters one's complacency; to allow ourselves to be baffled and humbled by the daily tasks of child care; and consciously to create a rhythm of meaningful activity, a place of devotion, a house of peace. But we must revive the art on a new footing.

The more women are welcomed into visible ministries and public involvements, and the more apparent it becomes that women are equal and gifted partners with men in all walks of life, and the more readily men demonstrate by their involvement that homemaking is worthy of a woman's and a man's active commitment—then, and now already, mature individuals will freely choose to stay home for a season.

"Homemaking means to build community with children and neighbors."

We must revive the vitality of the home or live with the deterioration brought on by a desperately ill life-support system. The true test of our liberation will be our ability to serve the least among us, without expecting much in return. "You were called to be free," proclaims Paul to the Galatians. "But do not use your freedom to indulge the sinful nature; rather, serve one another in love" (Galatians 5:13).

Like many other women of my generation, I have often been inspired by Luke's story of Jesus' encounter with Mary and Martha when Jesus commended Mary for sitting at his feet to listen. "Martha, Martha," the Lord answered, "you are worried and upset about many things, but only one thing is needed. Mary has chosen what is better, and it will not be taken away from her" (Luke 10:41-42). I imagined that by going to seminary I was becoming more like Mary, meriting Jesus' commendation for choosing what is better.

Sara Wenger Shenk is an author who writes about Christian issues. She lives in Yugoslavia.

"When parents come home from work in the evening, family times should emphasize sharing the experiences of the day."

Two-Career Couples Are Not Sacrificing Family Life

T. Berry Brazelton

The question I'm asked most frequently these days is, "Has child rearing changed since you started working with families in the 1950s?" I become almost speechless. The changes have been so great, and the new stresses on families so real and so apparent. What hasn't changed is the passion that parents have for doing a good job in raising their children. We in the '50s were passionate. But we were somber, undecided, retiring. We turned for advice to Dr. Spock. We brooded about whether we were doing the right things for our children.

The degree of stress that new parents feel about child rearing hasn't changed, but the focus for their anxiety has. We are in a period of real pressure on families. Parents have as much concern today about keeping the family together as in doing well by their children. At a time when nearly 50 percent of all marriages end up in divorce, maintaining family life is a high-risk venture. Single parents struggle against the dual demands of providing financial and emotional support for their children. Two-career couples face the conflicts of trying to balance work and family life—and trying to do both well.

These "new" families are searching for guidelines for rearing their children. As I talk with working parents around the country, they ask similar questions about how to cope with work and home—how to care for their children in a changing world, how to deal with the limited time they have for family life, how to live with the anxieties they have about child care, how to handle the inevitable competition they feel with their mates and caregivers. Yet for all their doubts and fears, there is a new force in the air that I feel in my contact with young families. The parents of this generation are beginning to feel empowered. They are asking hard

questions, demanding answers, and they are ready to fight for what they need for their children and for themselves. "Parent power" is the new catch phrase.

Working Women Need Support

In our culture, we live with a deep-seated view that a woman's role is in the home. She should be there for her children, so the theory goes, and both she and they will suffer if she's not. I felt that way for a long time myself, and it took constant badgering from my three militant daughters, who all work, as well as from a whole succession of working parents in my practice, to disabuse me of my set of mind. This bias prevents us from giving working women the support they need. It keeps us from realizing that 52 percent of women whose children are under 3 are in the work force, and it prevents us from providing them with choices for adequate child care. Many working women have no alternative but to leave their infants and small children in conditions none of us would trust. These women are as certain as you and I that their babies are at risk. But they have no choice.

Because of their double roles, women face a costly, necessary split within themselves. Can they invest themselves in a successful career and still be able to nurture a family? Can they cope with the guilt and the grief that they feel when they leave their children every day? Will women feel threatened as men get closer to the children? Their worries are understandable. A parent who must leave her small baby before she has completed her own work of attaching to him can't help but grieve. It's hard to free up energy for the workplace if a mother spends her time wondering whether her child is being adequately cared for. Women who choose to stay home with their children are equally conflicted. They wonder whether they should continue their careers out of self-protection—and whether the family can manage on one salary instead of two.

T. Berry Brazelton, "Working Parents," *Newsweek*, February 13, 1989. Reprinted with permission.

Upsetting as they may be, such concerns can be put to positive use. Women should allow themselves to feel anxious and guilty about leaving their children—those feelings will press them to find the best substitute care. Women can also find strength in their double roles. Lois Hoffman, a professor at the University of Michigan, has demonstrated in a study that working mothers who feel confident and fulfilled in their jobs bring that sense of competence home to their children.

Parent Rivalry

For men, greater involvement in the work of family life has forced them to confront the same conflicts women do—trying to balance working and caring. And as fathers accept nurturing roles within the family, competition with women is bound to emerge. There is an inevitable rivalry for the baby that will spring up between caring parents. Women may unconsciously act like "gatekeepers," excluding men from their babies' care. A new mother will say to her inexperienced, vulnerable husband, "Darling, that's not the way you diaper a baby!" or "You hold a baby *this* way." Working families need to be aware of this competition, which can disrupt family ties unless it is recognized. If parents can discuss it, the rivalry can motivate each person to become a better parent.

"The limited time [parents] have with their children makes each problem seem twice as difficult."

How can working men and women make the time they have with their children "quality time"? It's difficult when parents see their children for only an hour or two in the morning and a few hours in the evening. The whole concept of quality time can feel like a pressure. But if parents can concentrate on getting close to their children as soon as they walk in the door, then everything that follows becomes family time—working, playing, talking. Parents can involve children in their chores, teaching them to share the housework. Children who participate in the family's solutions will be competent to handle the stresses of their own generation. Even if time is short during workdays, parents can set aside time on the weekend for family celebration. Each parent should have a special time alone with each child at least once a week. An hour will do. But talk about it all week to remind the child—and yourself—that you will have a chance to cement your special relationship.

All parents worry about the same kinds of problems—sleep, feeding, toilet training, sibling rivalry. But there are some issues that seem especially troublesome for working parents, in part because the limited time they have with their children makes each problem seem twice as difficult. Some of the more perplexing issues—and suggestions for coping with them:

Going back to work: I am often asked when women should go back to work. I don't like to advocate one period of time over another, because for economic reasons some women don't have a choice about how long they can stay home. I am fighting for a four-month period of unpaid parental leave for both fathers and mothers, however, because I believe we must provide parents with the time to learn how to attach both to the baby and to each other. By 4 months, when colic has ended, and when the baby and parent know how to produce smiles and to vocalize for each other, the baby feels secure enough to begin turning away to look at other adults and to play with his own feet and his own toys. For the parent, it is marked by the sure knowledge that "he knows *me*. He will smile or vocalize at *me*."

Rx: Regardless of how much time new parents can take off from work, it's important to recognize that the process of learning to attach to a new infant is not a simple one. Everyone who holds a new baby falls in love. But while falling in love is easy, staying in love takes commitment. A newborn demands an inordinate amount of time and energy. He needs to be fed, changed, cuddled, carried and played with over endless 24-hour periods. He is likely to cry inconsolably every evening for the first 12 weeks. Much of the time his depressed, frightened parents are at a loss about what to do for him. A new mother will be dogged by postpartum blues; a new father is likely to feel helpless and want to run away. Their failures in this period are a major part of the process of learning to care. When new parents do not have the time and freedom to face this process and live through it successfully, they may indeed escape emotionally. In running away, they may miss the opportunity to develop a secure attachment to their baby—and never get to know themselves as real parents.

How To Deal with Pressure

Separation: Leave-taking in the morning can be a problem. Children will dawdle. They won't get dressed and they won't eat. Parents feel under pressure to get going; children resist this pressure. Everything goes to pot. The parent is faced with leaving a screaming child, and ends up feeling miserable all day.

Rx: Get up earlier. Sit down to talk or get close with the children before urging them to get dressed. Help them choose their clothes. Talk out the separation ahead. Remind them of the reunion at the end of the day. When you're ready to go, gather them up. Don't expect cooperation—the child is bound to be angry that you're leaving. And don't sneak out: always tell a child when you're going. Say goodbye and don't prolong your departure.

Discipline: The second most important parental job is discipline. Love comes first, but firm limits come second. A working parent feels too guilty and too tired to want to be tough at the end of the day. Of course parents would rather dodge the issue of being tough. But a child's agenda is likely to be different. When a child is falling apart, as children tend to do at the end of the day, he needs you most. He gets more frantic, searching for limits. Children need the security of boundaries, of knowing where they must stop.

Rx: Discipline should be seen as teaching rather than punishment. Taking time out, physically restraining and holding the child or isolating him for a brief period breaks the cycle. Immediately afterward parents can sit down and discuss the limits with firm assurance. No discipline works magically. Every episode is an opportunity to teach—but to teach *over time.* Working families need more organization than other families to make things work, and discipline gives a child a sense of being part of that organization.

Sleep issues: Separation during the day is so painful for working parents that separating at night becomes an even bigger issue, and putting their children to bed is fraught with difficulty. The normal teasing any child does about staying up is so stressful that working parents find it tough to be firm. Then a child's light-sleep episodes, which occur every three or five hours, become added conflicts. If the child cries out, parents often think they must go in to help her back into a deep sleep. But learning to sleep through the night is important for the child's own sense of independence.

"Discipline should be seen as teaching rather than punishment."

Rx: Teaching the child to get to sleep is the first goal. A child is likely to need a "lovey" or a comfort object, an independent resource to help her break the day-to-night transition. Learning to get herself to sleep means having a bedtime ritual that is soothing and comforting. But a child shouldn't fall asleep in her parent's arms; if she does, then the parents have made themselves part of the child's sleep ritual. Instead, after she's quiet, put her in bed with her lovey and pat her down to sleep. When she rouses every four hours, give her no more than five minutes to scrabble around in bed. Then go in and show her how to find her own comfort pattern for herself.

Feeding: Parents often believe that feeding is the major responsibility they have in taking care of their children. "If a child doesn't eat properly, it's the parent's fault," goes the myth. "A good parent gets a well-rounded diet into a child." Yet this myth ignores the child's need for autonomy in feeding. Each burst of independence hits feeding headlong, and food becomes a major issue. But because they are away most of the day, parents feel a need to become close to their children at mealtimes.

Rx: Try to ease up on the struggle. Leave as much as possible to the child. Steps to create autonomy in feeding: Start finger-feeding at 8 months. Let her make all of her own choices about what she'll eat by 1 year. Expect her to tease with food in the 2nd year. Set yourself easily attainable goals. If a child won't eat vegetables, give her a multivitamin every day. A simple amount of milk and protein covers her other needs for the short run. Most important, don't make food an issue. When parents come home from work in the evening, family time should emphasize sharing the experiences of the day, not eating. Your relationship is more important than the quantities of food consumed.

Competition with the Caregiver

Competition with the Caregiver: Every important area in child rearing—eating, discipline, toilet training—is likely to be a source of conflict between parents and caregivers. Both must recognize that the child's issues are ones of independence; the caregiver's, ones of control.

Rx: Conflict is inevitable. A child can adjust to two or even three different styles of child rearing if each of the adults really cares about him as an individual— and if parents and caregivers are in basic agreement on important issues. Differences in technique don't confuse a child—differences in basic values do.

Supermom and superbaby: People in conflict or under pressure dream about perfectionism. But trying to be perfect creates its own stresses. Any working mother is bound to blame any inadequacy in her own or her child's life on the fact that she's working. Being a perfect parent is not only an impossibility—it would be a disaster. Learning to be a parent is learning from mistakes.

Rx: Understand that there is no perfect way to be a parent. The myth of the supermom serves no real purpose except to increase the parent's guilt. And for children in working families, the pressures are already great. To expect them to be superbabies adds more pressure than they can face. Respect the child by understanding the demands she already faces in the normal stages of growing up. Teaching a child too early deprives her of her childhood. Play is the way a child learns and the way she sorts out what works for her. When she finds it on her own she gains a sense of competence.

We need a cushion for parents who are learning about their new job, to replace the role of the extended family when it is not available. When young parents are under stress—the normal stresses of childbearing and child rearing—they often don't know whom to turn to for help. If possible, I would prefer that grandparents be nearby and available. They can offer their own children a sense of security and support, which comes in handy at each new stress point. But parents often hesitate to turn to grandparents for advice. "They would tell me what to do, and I'd never do it that way" is a refrain I hear. My response is: "But if you know you'd 'never do it their way,' then you'd have a simpler decision to make."

Working men and women can also turn to other parents for support. Childbirth-education classes have been enormously valuable in helping parents face pregnancy and delivery successfully. Peer groups that provide support systems for parents are building on this model. Since its start 10 years ago, for example, The Family Resource Coalition in Chicago has been a drop-in center for single parents trying to raise their children alone in poorer sections of Chicago. There are similar centers across the United States for parents of all circumstances. Memberships in these groups can be counted in the hundreds of thousands. Special peer-support groups have been formed for parents of premature and high-risk babies; others have formed for the parents of almost every kind of impaired child.

What Can Be Done

Why haven't we done more as a nation to help working parents face the stresses of family life? We seem to be dominated by a bias left over from our pioneering ancestors: "Families should be self-sufficient. If they're not, they should suffer for it." Ironically, government help seems to increase families' dependency and insufficiency. As they are now configured, our government programs are available only to those who are willing to label themselves as failures—poor, hungry, uneducated, unmarried, single parents. This labeling produced the effect of giving up one's self-image. Labeled families become a self-fulfilling prophecy. We are reinforcing people not for success, but for failure.

Several of us have just formed a new grass-roots organization in Washington called Parent Action. This is a lobbying organization to demonstrate the energy that parents have. The organization of the American Association of Retired Persons has been successful in lobbying for the elderly. We want to push the concerns of families to the forefront of our nation's conscience.

So far, we in the United States have not even begun to address the burgeoning need for quality care for the children of working parents. We are the only industrialized country (aside from South Africa) that has not faced up to what is happening to young families as they try to cope with working and raising children. Indeed, our disappointing record in supporting families and children suggests that we are one of the least child-oriented societies in the world. The failure of the Alliance for Better Child Care, a bill sponsored by the Children's Defense Fund, a Washington-based advocacy group, represents just such an example. It would have provided national funds to increase the salaries of child-care workers so that trained personnel would have an incentive to care for infants and small children.

"Our disappointing record in supporting families and children suggests that we are one of the least child-oriented societies in the world."

In order to pay for the kind of care that every child deserves, the cost could be amortized four ways: by federal and state governments, by individual businesses and by the individual family. Business can play a key role. Offering employees parental leave, flexible work schedules and on-site or nearby day care would assure companies of a kind of allegiance that can be seen in European and Asian countries. Businesses that pay attention to the family concerns of their employees are already reaping rewards. Studies demonstrate that employees of such firms display less burnout, less absenteeism, more loyalty to the company and significantly more interest in their jobs.

As a nation, we have two choices. One is to continue to let our biases dominate our behavior as a society. The other is to see that we are a nation in crisis. We are spending billions of dollars to protect our families from outside enemies, imagined and real. But we do not have even 50 percent of the quality child care we need, and what we do have is neither affordable nor available to most families. These conditions exist in the face of all we know about the effects of emotional deprivation in early childhood. The rise in teenage suicide, pregnancies and crime should warn us that we are paying a dreadful price for not facing the needs of families early on. We are endangering both the present and the next generation.

T. Berry Brazelton is a clinical professor of pediatrics at Harvard Medical School in Cambridge, Massachusetts.

"Housework... is mostly boring, isolated, unpaid, pointless, [and] prevents one from doing anything else."

Family Responsibilities Limit Women's Career Opportunities

Debbie Taylor

In January 1973 a young criminal named Paul Giles was ordered by a UK [United Kingdom] magistrate to spring-clean an old-age pensioner's house as a punishment for his offence. On hearing this, women around the world might be forgiven for wondering just what heinous crimes *they* must have committed to justify their life sentences of cleaning.

But by equating it with a prison term, the magistrate showed a remarkable degree of insight into the nature of housework in modern society. It is mostly boring, isolated, unpaid, pointless, prevents one from doing anything else. . . . And there is no escape.

Cutlery, crockery, pots and pans rotate continuously from table to sink to draining board to cupboard and back to the table again. Clothes take similar round-trips from washing-basket to laundromat to ironing board to closet to washing-basket. Like convicts' work of digging holes then filling them in again, housework never ends and is never completed. Fifty years' hard labour, with no time off for good behaviour.

If this seems like an exaggeration, consider these statistics. In one US survey housewives were found to be doing an average of 99.6 hours' housework a week; UK mothers devote 50 hours a week just to child-care; in France and Sweden the number of hours spent on unpaid housework is greater than all the hours of paid employment put together. And of course the vast bulk of this labour is performed by women. In the US married men now do an impressive nine minutes more housework per day than they did 20 years ago, and in Italy 85 per cent of mothers with small children and full-time jobs outside the home are married to men who do no domestic work at all.

These are truly horrendous figures—enough to set many a feminist running amuck, Brillo pad and scrubbing-brush aloft, seeking some awful lingering vengeance. But wait. Doesn't 99.6 hours a week seem rather a lot for even the most house-proud housewife? What on earth are those women doing for 99.6 hours?

Doing Time

A great deal of unnecessary work, it seems. Research in the UK, for instance, found that the average toilet was scoured and the living-room carpet vacuumed four times a week. In fact women in Western societies are doing more housework now than ever before—60 hours a week in the EEC [European Economic Community] compared with between 46 and 52 hours half a century ago—despite the plethora of labour-saving devices that are now standard in many households.

You need only compare the hours full-time housewives put in with those done by neighbours who have jobs outside the home to see that a large proportion of this work is unnecessary. Data from 12 industrialized countries show that housewives do around 25 hours more housework per week than women with jobs. So clearly it is possible for a family to get by on the 31 hours a week done by the women with full-time jobs.

I do not want to imply here that the 99.6-hour housewives are incompetent or obsessional. Simply to suggest that housework is not merely a matter of supplying enough clean socks. It's about women providing the best possible *lifestyle* for their loved ones, in whatever time they have available. I will return to this later.

Meanwhile, let's look at those 31 hours the hard-pressed superwoman is forced to put in every week to keep the household running. Those hours of necessary but unpaid work are the main reason why men are the rulers of the world. It is as if women

Debbie Taylor, "Life Sentence: The Politics of Housework," *New Internationalist*, March 1988. Reprinted with permission from New Internationalist Publications.

have said: 'Here, I will give you 31 hours a week each, as a gift for you to use for earning money, furthering your careers, gaining power'.

The corollary, of course, is that women earn *less* money, sacrifice their careers, have little or no political power. It has been estimated, for instance, that UK women lost a total of $27 billion in overtime payments in 1987 because they had to leave work to rush to the shops, collect the children from school, prepare the evening meal. In the US only seven per cent of women workers are employed in managerial positions. And those few who do manage to achieve power and status must often do so at the expense of their private lives. Women professionals in the UK, for instance, are three times as likely as men professionals to be unmarried and childless.

In Marxist terms, women are not 'free' to sell their labour in the way that men are because the housework always comes first. Men are able to bargain with employers, offering to work shifts, say, in return for more money; or travelling to better-paid jobs in another part of the city. Women, on the other hand, gratefully accept any employment on offer that can somehow be dovetailed to fit in with their housework. This is why so many women work part-time—41 per cent of married women in the UK, for instance.

It is also one reason for the low pay of so-called 'pink-collar' occupations such as secretarial, clerical, nursing, catering and cleaning jobs, which are overwhelmingly done by women. In a mixed-sex group of workers, the demands of the men—with their greater 'freedom' of labour and bargaining power—will tend to push everyone's basic wage up. But when all the workers are women they are far easier to exploit.

Natural Victims

And when the work they do for wages is so similar to the work they do for nothing in their homes, their bargaining power is further undercut by the assumption that their work is 'natural' and therefore unskilled. In fact the exact opposite might well be the case: that men's *lack* of skills like dexterity, patience and empathy—required for so many pink-collar occupations—means women are the only people able to do such jobs. But these skills are not reflected in the wages: in the US, where 80 per cent of working women are employed in clerical work of some kind, a secretary with 18 years experience still earns less than a parking-lot attendant.

These, then, are the consequences of that gift of 31 hours a week: power and wealth for men; responsibility and poverty for women. And individual husbands are not the only ones to profit from the domestic slavery of their wives. It has been estimated, for instance, that companies would have to add around 30 per cent to their wage bills if they were to pay women fairly for the paid work they do. And if governments had to fork out for the *unpaid* work as well, the amount of money that would change hands would add up to around 40 per cent of GNP [gross national product]. In the US the amount theoretically owed each year to women for unpaid domestic work is six times the annual military budget.

"Individual husbands are not the only ones to profit from the domestic slavery of their wives."

If you had not already begun to smell a rat, then the whiff should be getting through to you about now. Because this state of affairs clearly did not come about by accident. Women in the industrialized world did not gather together over tea one afternoon and agree to work unpaid for those 31 hours out of the sheer kindness of their hearts. No, they were given little choice. They were, as Ivan Illich put it, 'flattered and threatened, by capitalist and cleric' into their current situation.

A number of authors have investigated the history of housework and have discovered that, though domestic work has existed ever since there was a *domus* in which to do it, the housewife role is a very recent one indeed—and confined to industrialized societies. As sociologist Anne Oakley put it: 'other cultures may live in families but they do not necessarily have housewives'. They have women, men and children whose labour is woven together like coloured thread in a tapestry, creating home, life and livelihood for the whole family.

A woman in Kenya starts to untie the shawl securing her baby to her back, so she can wield her hoe with more freedom among the maize stalks. Before her hands have loosened the knot, another child's willing arms will be waiting to take the baby from her. While she works, the hoe flashing in the sunshine, her daughters will be pounding sorghum and fetching water for the evening meal, her sons driving goats and cattle to fresh grazing, her husband sinking wooden poles into the ground for a new house.

Growing Food and Children

All of these activites are work, but those that we would term housework are so intricately interwoven with agriculture that it is difficult to tease them apart. The growing of food and the growing of children are both vital to the family's survival. Without children the food cannot be grown; without food there can be no children. Who would dare make the judgement that holding your youngest baby on your lap and coaxing her to eat her first mouthful of porridge is less important than weeding a few more yards in the maize field?

Yet this is the judgement our society makes constantly. Production—of nails, televisions, canned soup, Wrangler jeans—is important. Reproduction—Marx's term for that work of cleaning, feeding and caring that begets children and rekindles workers' energy at the end of each day—is unimportant. How did this degradation of reproduction or domestic work come about? And how is it that women in our societies are expected to manage it alone?

Well, according to Oakley, Illich and many others, the domestic rot set in (along with many other kinds of rot) with the growth of the cities, factories and mines of early capitalism. By 1850 half of the UK population were living in cities. In those days factory and mine-owners did not care who did their work for them and hired whole families to dig coal or weave cloth in the textile mills. It might have continued that way, too, except for two main things.

First was the extraordinarily high infant mortality rate in the dreadful city slums where the workers lived. This came about largely because domestic work among the new proletariat had been reduced to an absolute minimum, crowded out by the demands of wage labour. Reproduction was no longer as vital for survival as it had been when families lived off the land. So babies were left untended in filthy hovels with no water or sanitation and weaned onto gruel as soon as they were born, to free their mothers for work in the factories. In fact the general 'condition of the working class' became a cause for serious concern among capitalists. Malnourished, disease-ridden, stunted and crippled by the conditions in which they lived, the workers were less and less able to do a good day's work. Epidemics of diphtheria and typhoid swept through the slums like evil floodwater and began to lap at the doors of the rich.

Meanwhile the clatter of the tumbrels in the stinking streets was drowned out by the roar of ever-more efficient machinery in the factories. And the more efficient the machines became, the fewer the workers that were needed to work them.

Redundant Wives

At this point the story starts to read like a conspiracy—though in fact capitalism tends to operate more by trial and error, rather like Darwinian evolution, with the 'fittest' (by which I mean the most cost-effective for capitalists) economic arrangements surviving. It turned out that the most cost-effective way to run a workforce was to throw women out of the factories and put them to work on improving the lamentable 'condition of the working class' in their homes. This had the added advantage that only one wage-packet would need to be paid—to the man of the house—to support the working-class family.

Both women and men protested vigorously: the women because they were accustomed to providing for themselves; the men because they resented being made suddenly responsible for their wives and children (compulsory education for children and restrictive employment laws had barred children, too, from the factories by this time). 'The plebeians rioted,' says Illich. 'And the crowd was led, more often than not, by its women'.

The rioting went on until what Illich mischievously calls 'the enclosure of women'—the transformation of women into housewives—was completed. In 1737 over 98 per cent of married women in England worked outside the home. By 1911 over 90 per cent were employed solely as housewives. And this pattern was repeated throughout the industrialized world.

"We are trained for our servile role from the day we are born."

The means by which this 'enclosure of women' was effected were many and various. There was the 'germ theory' of disease, for example, which led well-heeled hypochondriachal do-gooders to take the gospel of 'domestic science' to the masses. Annual spring-cleaning became a thing of the past as women were exhorted to rid their homes of 'germ-infested dust'. Doctors and scientists reinforced the laws preventing women working and confirmed their economically-dependent status by 'discovering' women's 'natural' sensitivity and fragility. Religious authorities weighed in too, urging these tender-hearted creatures to be the guarantors of their husband's and children's morality.

Divide and Rule

Perhaps if women had had the support of their men from the beginning, they might have been able to resist these pressures on them to provide free domestic services. But the capitalists had effected a split between working-class men and women by, as Illich puts it, 'making working men wardens of their domestic women, one on one, and making this guardianship into a burdensome duty'. A similar antagonism between the sexes can be observed today in developing countries where the introduction of cash crops and wage-labour has given men—but not women—access to money. The men feel the money is theirs; the women resent their lack of control over the family's income.

Today the carrots and sticks used latterly to force women into domestic slavery are no longer necessary. We are trained for our servile role from the day we are born. So powerful is our training that even the massive influx of women back into the labour force in recent years has had practically no effect on the division of labour in our homes.

This is because, as I mentioned earlier, women are trained to *take care* of their loved ones. This means that the housewife role includes much more than the sheer drudgery of providing clean socks. It is also a cool hand on a feverish forehead in the early hours; boiling his eggs exactly the way he likes them; flowers on the table; organizing a treasure hunt for Easter-eggs. . . . Domestic labour has become fused in our minds with love—which is why some housewives work a 99.6 hour week and why a woman's work is literally never done. What woman would put a ceiling on love?

It is probably not necessary to point out here that *men* do not appear to have the same problem with limiting their devotion. While this is lamentable in many ways, there is a part (a very small part) of me that sympathizes with them.

Cooking and Caring

Men perceive the trap that the conflation of love and domestic work comprises. They fear that to place even one toe over the edge would send them hurtling into the bottomless pit of self-sacrifice that is women's current caring role. As soon as they do attempt a smidgin of housework, they often find themselves caught up in a wrangle about 'standards'—a wrangle which is really about deciding when enough is enough. If housework really were only about providing clean socks, then men *might* be more prepared to do their share.

"We should stop equating loving with unpaid domestic service."

Women have to unpick this tangle of finite domestic labour and infinite love. Because it is a tangle that ensnares us as surely as any fly in a web. This is not to suggest that we should stop loving. Just that we should stop equating loving with unpaid domestic service as if the two were interchangeable. Ironing shirts yet more perfectly does not increase the sum of human happiness. In fact there is some evidence that the opposite is the case: that children are more likely to become delinquent, babies and women more likely to be battered, in homes where women are full-time housewives.

Having disentangled cooking from caring, the next step is to apportion the cooking equally among all who benefit from it. In heterosexual households the agenda is clear: otherwise one person's leisure and advancement is bought at the *direct* expense of the other's toil and stagnation. If you have children, ensure that they start doing their share of the chores too—as early as possible (bearing in mind that many Third World children are working in the fields, cooking meals *and* going to school by the age of nine).

The key, then, is to eschew all unreciprocated domestic labour. This includes paying for the labour of a nanny, child-minder or cleaner. After all, who cleans the cleaner's house or minds the child-minder's children? Not her (*sic*) employers, that's for sure. And the existence of single mothers or families on the lowest of low incomes means that the middle-class couple's solution of sharing the chores or passing the buck onto someone else will simply not work. Not every woman has a male partner available (let alone willing) to share the housework. Not every family can afford to pay for other people to do it for them.

This may sound utopian (I don't know about you, but I have nothing against utopias), but if housework were organized on a simple basis of equal distribution, then both rich and poor people, single parents and married couples, adults and children would all become equally tied to (and equally freed from) the home. And women's 50 years' of hard labour, in solitary confinement, could be commuted to a suspended sentence.

Debbie Taylor writes for New Internationalist, *a British magazine which focuses on world poverty and development.*

*"There is no reason why a woman should
not be able to realize her ambition...
for both the personal and professional
sides of life."*

viewpoint **10**

Family Responsibilities Do Not Limit Women's Career Opportunities

Gay Sheldon Goldman with Kate Kelly

Although over 50 percent of all women with children under six are currently in the work force, the question of how to balance child-rearing responsibilities, marriage, household duties, and paid employment continues to plague young mothers. Guilt, self-doubt, and stress from both home and work abound. In spite of the vast inroads made in the workplace toward gender equality, the career-family dilemma largely remains a female problem.

"I am in constant turmoil—never knowing where to put my primary energy," states a 32-year-old bank vice president with two toddlers. "But my identity—who I am—is tied up in what I do. I'd be afraid to quit."

"'Mommy stay home! Mommy stay home!' pleads my two-and-a-half-year-old as I leave the apartment each morning," says a 40-year-old CEO [Chief Executive Officer]. "It fills me with guilt and misgivings."

Another young mother recalls, "No one at Stanford ever thought I would leave the job market. But after we adopted Laurie, there was a radical change in me. I went back to my 'glamorous,' high-paying job after six months, but it was no good. I wanted to be with that wonderful baby I had yearned for so badly. I left, and I know I did the right thing. Fortunately, I had the choice."

"Sure my husband helps out," answers a pregnant attorney, who recently cut back her workload. "He says, 'Just *tell* me what to do and I'll do it.' All the managing, meal planning, appointment making, and crisis intervention still falls on me. Frankly, I'm better at it, but it takes *time*."

Questions and Doubt

Conflict. You hear it all around. While most women are more than happy to acknowledge that Superwoman is a myth, what they are looking for in

life is what men have always hoped for: a family, challenging work, and just compensation for the job they do. Yet one picks up spoken and unspoken feelings of doubt: "If I continue to work, am I doing a disservice to my children?" "If I take time off and stay at home, will I ever be able to rebuild a successful career?" "Does it matter if I'm not there for class trips and PTA meetings?" "Why am I always the one who stays home if the kids are sick?" "And what about *me*? Whether I'm at home or working at the office, I feel torn apart. . . ."

What is not being conveyed to today's young female achiever is that there *are* alternate ways to "have it all," to realize one's ambition for the personal as well as the professional. What's more, in women a half-generation ahead of today's young careerists there exists a whole spectrum of positive role models.

While today's young woman wonders whether (and how) to incorporate children into her professional life, the woman who came of age in the late 1950's and early 1960's was in conflict over how (and whether) to incorporate work into her family-oriented life. Now the primary difference between the generations is that the older women are far enough along to see the consequences of the decisions they've made.

A few years ago, before the myth of Supermom was exposed, I chose to leave a position I greatly enjoyed in an organization I helped create. I found I could no longer juggle the needs and unpredictable demands of a rapidly growing regional theater company with the needs and demands of three young children, a husband, and a home. Naturally, I wondered if my crisis was a personal failure or if burnout was a widespread problem among ambitious, but nurturing, women.

My interest in the subject coincided with the planning of my twenty-fifth college reunion, and I used the opportunity to find out how my classmates

Gay Sheldon Goldman with Kate Kelly, "Choices of the Modern Mother," *Parents* magazine, October 1988. Reprinted with permission.

nationwide were faring. With the aid of a sociologist and several other advisors, I conducted a class survey and then continued the study with a much broader segment of educated women.

As I analyzed the material gathered from over 300 college-educated women from all regions of the country and from diverse socioeconomic backgrounds, seven distinguishable life patterns began to emerge. Three of them—the Supermom (3 percent of those studied), the married woman who works full-time and carries full responsibilities for home and family as well; the Floater (2 percent), who drifts from job to job while waiting for her destined mate to materialize; and the Displaced Homemaker (9 percent), divorced women who were raised under one set of ground rules and divorced under another (often emotionally and financially battered)—presented troublesome role models.

However, among the four remaining life patterns—the Traditionalist (23 percent), the Adapter (34 percent), the Parallel Participant (18 percent), and the Self-Sufficient Single (11 percent)—I was able to find answers. The majority of the women in these categories—65 percent of all the women studied—had found healthy, dynamic solutions to the career-family dilemma.

"The 'empty nest' syndrome is becoming outdated."

Most of these women were "having it all" not simultaneously, but serially, in stages of accomplishment. Many had moved from part-time positions to full-time employment, had switched to more challenging careers in male-dominated fields, or had joined the workforce in unconventional ways and at untraditional ages. In their late forties and early fifties, these women felt very positive about their lives. Those with no major health problems seemed to be experiencing a period of intense satisfaction at being able to devote time to their own needs after years of nurturing others. Based on an examination of these women, one would conclude that now that women have more options, the "empty nest" syndrome is becoming outdated. The women studied had a strong vision of the future—and looked forward to climbing exciting new mountains in terms of personal growth, careers, and community service over the *next* 25 years.

Here is a look at how these women, ranging from the very traditional to the quite modern, made their lives work.

Unlike the traditional homemaker of Betty Friedan's *The Feminine Mystique*, who was resentful of her dependence upon a male breadwinner and unfulfilled by her lack of paid employment, the Traditionalist by Choice has carefully weighed the pros and cons of paid employment and still opts to be the primary care-giver, pursuing volunteer activities that are compatible with family needs. She doesn't mourn the path not taken but functions contentedly within a marriage based on financial and political equality. Whether she's a farmer's wife with five children who voluntarily teaches local children about animals or an organization leader whose decisions have a profound impact on local school systems, art organizations, or politics, the Traditionalist by Choice needs to contribute, to make a difference. States one school board president: "I have no regrets about my volunteer activities and the extraordinary opportunities I have had to make a difference in the quality of life for my family and for the city."

For many, this lifestyle is only a temporary career break during part of the child-rearing years. Some of our most notable public figures—Sandra Day O'Connor, Jeane Kirkpatrick, Geraldine Ferraro—gave up paid employment for a number of years to raise young children.

For other women, this way of life is a long-term commitment, though not necessarily a permanent one. "I don't just fit my husband and three teenagers into a busy schedule," relates a remarried ex-careerist. "I chose to give them prime time." For Beatrice Guthrie, her many years volunteering as a prime fund-raiser for the Metropolitan Opera offered adequate time for her husband and three school-age children as well as an opportunity to learn fund-raising techniques. It also allowed for considerable intellectual growth. "As I researched each new production, I was continuously getting an education in classical music and history. The position put me in contact with the finest opera conductors and artists, and it gave me the opportunity to use different foreign languages. I kept fairly regular hours—but I didn't *have* to stick to a schedule if I had an overriding personal commitment."

The Adapter

The Adapter works *paid* employment around the needs and schedule of her family. Although like the Traditionalist by Choice she accepts and enjoys the role of nurturer, values her marriage, and is willing to accommodate the reasonable needs of a major breadwinner, she has, or develops, an acute need to achieve within the paid work force—either because extra income is needed by the family or because she seeks the feeling of accomplishment and self-worth a paycheck can bring. Her goal is to successfully integrate paid employment with her top priority, a family-oriented life. She does this by pursuing career paths that are outside the structured nine-to-five work force, by working part-time, in a flexible full-time job, or as a free-lancer. "I need measurable success in the competitive marketplace where a paycheck is your report card," explains Susan, a

50-year-old wife and mother of three. Since her youngest child turned eleven, she has worked on a flexible schedule as a real estate agent, averaging an annual six-figure salary.

For Laura, who is married to an attorney and is the mother of two sons, finding the right career path was a matter of trial and error. In the mid-1970's, pressured by what she felt was a need to achieve in a "man's world," Laura entered business school. "I was taking a mid-term, and I realized that I hated it. I'd hated business school from the day I started. I thought, this is going to be the hardest thing I've done in my life, but I'm going to quit." After coming to terms with her true interests and needs, Laura, through a combination of luck, perseverance, and hard work, was able to turn her knowledge and love of art history into a paying occupation. She is now doing what she enjoys—working as a part-time staff lecturer at an outstanding Midwestern museum and organizing art tours and lectures for organizations on a free-lance basis.

"Some of our most notable public figures—Sandra Day O'Connor, Jeane Kirkpatrick, Geraldine Ferraro—gave up paid employment for a number of years to raise young children."

The Adapter's way of integrating work and family has been the most popular one among women educated in the 1950's. It is a natural solution for achievement-oriented women whose husbands are the primary breadwinners. It allows a wife and mother an opportunity to create or maintain a position in the working world while still occupying the role of primary care-giver—a role that these women did not *wish* to give up. (In some modern families, it is the husband who is assuming the role of the Adapter, while the wife remains the primary breadwinner.)

For some Adapters, this way of integrating career and family represents an interim measure. When family responsibilities lessen or the children leave, they choose to give full reign to their ambition by joining the full-time structured work force. But for others, the Adapter's approach represents a long-term solution, allowing them the flexibility and freedom to take vacations and business trips with their husbands and to spend time with friends, adult children, and grandchildren, all while remaining a part of the working world.

The Self-Sufficient Single Parent has children but no husband to work into the equation. She is usually committed to functioning within the nine-to-five, structured work force. Her self-sufficiency is generally unplanned, resulting from a need to replace the primacy of a marital relationship with meaningful work. Unlike the Displaced Homemaker, who finds it extremely difficult to move on with her life, the Self-Sufficient Single, although often strained by single parenthood, has found a stimulating occupation, has grown in her own right, and has built a supportive network of friends to replace the primacy of the mate.

Tamara did not work for pay during her marriage. The difficult task of retraining for a career and interviewing for a job at 40 became essential when her marginal marriage came to an end after fourteen years. "The seven years since my divorce are the most clearly etched in my memory, since this is the period in which I grew up, belatedly, and took control of my life," said Tamara, who is now a securities analyst.

In contrast, Katherine, a successful corporate executive, was among those who were well prepared for forging ahead on their own. "I always assumed I would do something," she reflects. "I thought a lot about success. I wanted to be important." Throughout her married life, she made a serious commitment to both her children and her career, taking only a brief time off after the birth of each child. "I found that when you're home, the world insists on coming to talk to you. If you're there, the repairman, who can perfectly well fix the light fixture in the kitchen without you, has to talk to you. Second, I was running up and down stairs all day, so I was medically better off in the office," she continues. "What you really need to do is organize a household in a way that is predictable for the baby, so that the child grows up feeling self-confident and secure. The reason people have a problem is that they have stayed home for four months and then go back to work. They are abandoning the baby just at the time the child is becoming aware of abandonment. You change the routine at the same time that human beings need more structure."

The Parallel Participant

The Parallel Participant greatly values her role as wife and mother but also needs and enjoys full-time work in the structured work force. Many of these women reentered the work force or increased their commitment to it after taking time out for child rearing.

The Parallel Participant usually shares domestic responsibilities with her mate (not like Supermom who assumes the full burden of care-giving and full-time employment). "I entered law school when my youngest [of three children] started the first grade," states Florence. "After passing the bar exam, I was hired by a firm in our medium-size town and five years later was made a partner. It wasn't easy, but none of this would have been possible without the emotional support and physical help of my husband."

Florence's way of entering the established work force is not unique. Most Parallel Participants educated in the 1950's entered or reentered the world of work in untraditional ways. Some retrained for a mature entry into the professions or attended a professional school in their thirties or forties after starting or raising a family. Sara Dawson started business school at 40, then entered a bank training program, and is now a vice president. Barbara Black, equipped with a law degree, took time off the career track for nine years while raising three children. She gradually retooled for an academic career (acquiring a Ph.D. in history) and became a full-time, tenured assistant professor at Yale in 1976. She is now dean of the Columbia Law School.

Other Parallel Participants put skills acquired as volunteers and household managers to use in government positions, hospital and school administration, and corporate managerial positions. Suzi Oppenheimer, wife and mother of four grown children, is a good example. She moved from a volunteer position as president of the League of Women Voters to mayor of Mamaroneck, New York, and is now serving her second term as a state senator.

Still others look at the big picture and discover a need. With abundant energy, resourcefulness, and a willingness to take risks, many 1950's women have developed successful businesses ranging from financial planning services and art galleries to production companies and retailing. "When my youngest child was two, I began to bother everyone I knew about what I should do," recalled one successful entrepreneur. "I was going to open a boutique or bake pies, but then somebody suggested that since my previous work experience had been with a magazine, I should start a regional publication. There were three women in the room, and the three of us decided to do it. We sold it for a substantial profit in 1981, and a year later, I started a financial newsletter that now has a large national subscription base."

Lessons To Live By

In order to integrate the personal and professional in their lives successfully, these pre-baby-boom women had to be aware of their own needs and temperaments; they had to understand the nature of their trade-offs and trust that, over time, they would be able to accomplish all of the goals that were important to them. There are lessons in their lives for mothers today. Specifically:

There is no one way, or right way, to be an educated woman in our society. In spite of media hype and its profound influence on all of us, there is a wide spectrum of choices for combining love and work.

The traditionally "male" path to success need not be the only one. Almost all of the women took career detours along the way. Most say, looking back, that the detours provided personal enrichment they would have missed had they focused solely on work throughout their lives.

Equality is necessary within a loving relationship. In successful marriages, financial and political equity are implicit in the partnership even if the wife and husband choose to assume different financial and care-giving roles.

Time invested in child rearing pays off, in most cases, with substantial dividends. The joys of motherhood have given unparalleled satisfaction to the great majority; 90 percent of the women would have as many or more children. They now see their offspring as charming, well-adjusted young adults.

"The traditionally 'male' path to success need not be the only one."

Financially rewarding, fulfilling work, or a strong commitment to a volunteer cause is a top priority. As the nest empties, meaningful work outside family concerns is important for one's well-being. The women in the study who expressed the most discontent with their lives lacked this orientation.

It is evident that educated wives and mothers will continue to move in and out of the work force, and probably within it, with much greater frequency than men. Society must keep striving for ways to accommodate women's different work patterns, due to mothering, and embrace the concept of serial stages of accomplishment. With the gift of extended life that medical science has given us, there is no reason why a woman should not be able to realize her ambition, whatever it may be, for both the personal and professional sides of life.

Gay Sheldon Goldman is a free-lance writer and theater producer. Kate Kelly is a free-lance writer.

"The career-and-family woman is willing to trade off the pressures and demands that go with promotion for the freedom to spend more time with her children."

viewpoint **11**

A "Mommy Track" for Working Mothers Is Beneficial

Felice N. Schwartz

The cost of employing women in management is greater than the cost of employing men. This is a jarring statement, partly because it is true, but mostly because it is something people are reluctant to talk about. A new study by one multinational corporation shows that the rate of turnover in management positions is 2½ times higher among top-performing women than it is among men. A large producer of consumer goods reports that one-half of the women who take maternity leave return to their jobs late or not at all. And we know that women also have a greater tendency to plateau or to interrupt their careers in ways that limit their growth and development. But we have become so sensitive to charges of sexism and so afraid of confrontation, even litigation, that we rarely say what we know to be true. Unfortunately, our bottled-up awareness leaks out in misleading metaphors ("glass ceiling" is one notable example), veiled hostility, lowered expectations, distrust, and reluctant adherence to Equal Employment Opportunity requirements.

Career interruptions, plateauing, and turnover are expensive. The money corporations invest in recruitment, training, and development is less likely to produce top executives among women than among men, and the invaluable company experience that developing executives acquire at every level as they move up through management ranks is more often lost.

The studies just mentioned are only the first of many, I'm quite sure. Demographic realities are going to force corporations all across the country to analyze the cost of employing women in managerial positions, and what they will discover is that women cost more.

But here is another startling truth: The greater cost of employing women is not a function of inescapable gender differences. Women *are* different from men, but what increases their cost to the corporation is principally the clash of their perceptions, attitudes, and behavior with those of men, which is to say, with the policies and practices of male-led corporations.

It is terribly important that employers draw the right conclusions from the studies now being done. The studies will be useless—or worse, harmful—if all they teach us is that women are expensive to employ. What we need to learn is how to reduce that expense, how to stop throwing away the investments we make in talented women, how to become more responsive to the needs of the women that corporations *must* employ if they are to have the best and the brightest of all those now entering the work force. . . .

Career-First Women

There is no question that the management ranks of business will include increasing numbers of women. There remains, however, the question of how these women will succeed—how long they will stay, how high they will climb, how completely they will fulfill their promise and potential, and what kind of return the corporation will realize on its investment in their training and development.

There is ample business reason for finding ways to make sure that as many of these women as possible will succeed. The first step in this process is to recognize that women are not all alike. Like men, they are individuals with differing talents, priorities, and motivations. For the sake of simplicity, let me focus on . . . what I call the career-primary woman and the career-and-family woman.

Like many men, some women put their careers first. They are ready to make the same trade-offs traditionally made by the men who seek leadership positions. They make a career decision to put in extra hours, to make sacrifices in their personal lives, to make the most of every opportunity for professional development. For women, of course, this decision also requires that they remain single or at least childless or, if they do have children, that they be satisfied to have others raise them. Some 90% of executive men but only 35% of executive women have children by the age of 40. The *automatic* association of all women with babies is clearly unjustified.

The secret to dealing with such women is to recognize them early, accept them, and clear artificial barriers from their path to the top. After all, the best of these women are among the best managerial talent you will ever see. And career-primary women have another important value to the company that men and other women lack. They can act as role models and mentors to younger women who put their careers first. Since upwardly mobile career-primary women still have few role models to motivate and inspire them, a company with women in its top echelon has a significant advantage in the competition for executive talent.

Men at the top of the organization—most of them over 55, with wives who tend to be traditional—often find career women "masculine" and difficult to accept as colleagues. Such men miss the point, which is not that these women are just like men but that they are just like the *best* men in the organization. And there is such a shortage of the best people that gender cannot be allowed to matter. It is clearly counterproductive to disparage in a woman with executive talent the very qualities that are most critical to the business and that might carry a man to the CEO's office.

"There is such a shortage of the best people that gender cannot be allowed to matter."

Clearing a path to the top for career-primary women has four requirements:

1. Identify them early.

2. Give them the same opportunity you give to talented men to grow and develop and contribute to company profitability. Give them client and customer responsibility. Expect them to travel and relocate, to make the same commitment to the company as men aspiring to leadership positions.

3. Accept them as valued members of your management team. Include them in every kind of communication. Listen to them.

4. Recognize that the business environment is more difficult and stressful for them than for their male peers. They are always a minority, often the only woman. The male perception of talented, ambitious women is at best ambivalent, a mixture of admiration, resentment, confusion, competitiveness, attraction, skepticism, anxiety, pride, and animosity. Women can never feel secure about how they should dress and act, whether they should speak out or grin and bear it when they encounter discrimination, stereotyping, sexual harassment, and paternalism. Social interaction and travel with male colleagues and with male clients can be charged. As they move up, the normal increase in pressure and responsibility is compounded for women because they are women.

Stereotypical language and sexist day-to-day behavior do take their toll on women's career development. Few male executives realize how common it is to call women by their first names while men in the same group are greeted with surnames, how frequently female executives are assumed by men to be secretaries, how often women are excluded from all-male social events where business is being transacted. With notable exceptions, men are still generally more comfortable with other men, and as a result women miss many of the career and business opportunities that arise over lunch, on the golf course, or in the locker room.

Career-and-Family Women

The majority of women, however, are what I call career-and-family women, women who want to pursue serious careers while participating actively in the rearing of children. These women are a precious resource that has yet to be mined. Many of them are talented and creative. Most of them are willing to trade some career growth and compensation for freedom from the constant pressure to work long hours and weekends.

Most companies today are ambivalent at best about the career-and-family women in their management ranks. They would prefer that all employees were willing to give their all to the company. They believe it is in their best interests for all managers to compete for the top positions so the company will have the largest possible pool from which to draw its leaders.

"If you have both talent and motivation," many employers seem to say, "we want to move you up. If you haven't got that motivation, if you want less pressure and greater flexibility, then you can leave and make room for a new generation." These companies lose on two counts. First, they fail to amortize the investment they made in the early training and experience of management women who find themselves committed to family as well as to career. Second, they fail to recognize what these women could do for their middle management.

The ranks of middle managers are filled with people on their way up and people who have stalled. Many of them have simply reached their limits, achieved career growth commensurate with or exceeding their capabilities, and they cause problems because their performance is mediocre but they still want to move ahead. The career-and-family woman is willing to trade off the pressures and demands that go with promotion for the freedom to spend more time with her children. She's very smart, she's talented, she's committed to her career, and she's satisfied to stay at the middle level, at least during the early child-rearing years. Compare her with some of the people you have there now.

Still a Major Player

Consider a typical example, a woman who decides in college on a business career and enters management at age 22. For nine years, the company invests in her career as she gains experience and skills and steadily improves her performance. But at 31, just as the investment begins to pay off in earnest, she decides to have a baby. Can the company afford to let her go home, take another job, or go into business for herself? The common perception now is yes, the corporation can afford to lose her unless, after six or eight weeks or even three months of disability and maternity leave, she returns to work on a full-time schedule with the same vigor, commitment, and ambition that she showed before.

"The high-performing career-and-family woman can be a major player in your company."

But what if she doesn't? What if she wants or needs to go on leave for six months or a year or, heaven forbid, five years? In this worst-case scenario, she works full-time from age 22 to 31, and from 36 to 65—a total of 38 years as opposed to the typical male's 43 years. That's not a huge difference. Moreover, my typical example is willing to work part-time while her children are young, if only her employer will give her the opportunity. There are two rewards for companies responsive to this need: higher retention of their best people and greatly improved performance and satisfaction in their middle management.

The high-performing career-and-family woman can be a major player in your company. She can give you a significant business advantage as the competition for able people escalates. Sometimes too, if you can hold on to her, she will switch gears in mid-life and reenter the competition for the top. The price you must pay to retain these women is threefold: you must plan for and manage maternity, you must provide the flexibility that will allow them to be maximally productive, and you must take an active role in helping to make family supports and high-quality, affordable child care available to all women.

Felice N. Schwartz is president and founder of Catalyst, a nonprofit organization that works with corporations to develop the careers and leadership potential of women.

"Anyone who juggles work and children learns things about management that make the Harvard Business School seem like kindergarten."

A "Mommy Track" for Working Mothers Is Unnecessary

Abigail Trafford

When it comes to management skills, what you need on your résumé may not be an MBA, but a baby. Because anyone who juggles work and children learns things about management that make the Harvard Business School seem like kindergarten.

That's why today's working mothers may be among the top managers of corporate America in the 1990s. In their struggle to combine job and children, they are learning the crucial modern management skills—of using time efficiently, setting priorities, making decisions, developing staff and handling crises.

This notion, of course, runs counter to the current argument about the need for a special "Mommy Track" in major corporations and law firms. The debate was triggered by an article in the *Harvard Business Review* by Felice N. Schwartz, the head of Catalyst, a nonprofit organization that helps women advance their careers. She points out that the cost of employing women in management is greater than the cost of employing men because some women drop out (or plateau out) at work after they have children. She advises corporations to divide women into two separate and unequal classes: the career-primary women who remain single or at least childless and the career-and-family women who mix children with the job.

Experience the Hard Way

The first group should be encouraged to pursue the Fast Track and aim for the A-Team in corporate management. But most women, she writes, are on the Mommy Track and "are willing to trade some career growth and compensation for freedom from the constant pressure to work long hours and weekends." In other words, these women should settle for the B-Team, which translates into lower expectations, less pay and a nice dead-end job in middle management.

This two-track approach for women has been hailed by some business leaders as a first step toward getting some truths about working mothers out of the closet. But to many of us who have pursued a career and raised children, it seems like a phony debate—and one that shortchanges the special skills many women have acquired.

What distorts the argument is the definition of experience, which over a lifetime encompasses much more than the number of hours spent in the office. Those of us who have traveled the career and family tracks simultaneously have gained experience the hard way.

To be sure, not all working mothers make good managers (or good parents). And a person doesn't have to raise children to learn how to manage people. But many of the challenges managers face in running a company are similar to what parents face in raising a family.

Here are one 48-year-old working woman's 10 rules for modern mommy (and daddy) managers:

• Be ruthless about time. Time is the most precious commodity for working parents. When you integrate the full-time demands of a job with those of raising a family, you end up with a Personal Time Deficit that forces you to eliminate all nonessential activities.

In most companies, people spend a certain percentage of the day doing la-la-la work: that is, hanging out by the coffee pot, grazing through extended "business" lunches, giving meetings on issues peripheral to the job at hand, gossiping in and out of the office. A little bit of la-la-la can be chalked up to office politics and a healthy mental break from job pressures. But that kind of unfocused cruising is the first thing to go for working mothers. "I never do lunches," says Bonnie Cohen, 46, senior vice president at the National Trust for Historic

Abigail Trafford, "The Mommy Track Should Be the Road to Top Management," *The Washington Post National Weekly Edition*, April 10-16, 1989. © The Washington Post.

Preservation, who has two children—one in college, the other in fifth grade. "I try to go to as few meetings as I can."

"I used to spend a lot of time schmoozing with people—amazing how much time I spent," says Jamie Gorelick, 38, a partner in the Washington law firm of Miller, Cassidy, Larroca & Lewin, who has a young baby at home. "You learn to value time differently and get the most out of it." Before the baby, Gorelick was at the office from 8 a.m. to 7 p.m. and working evenings and weekends. Now her hours are 9:15 to 6 and she rarely works on weekends. "It's not the same full time, but I would be surprised if my productivity the way law firms measure it has dropped in any noticeable manner."

The Cocker Spaniel Story

• Set priorities. The only way to hold down the Time Deficit is to identify and follow a limited number of primary goals that you can manage at this stage in your life. That means just saying no to the tidal wave of demands—not just from the job, but from the community and home as well. For Gorelick, it means turning down requests for speeches and articles. For Wendy Crisp, 45, the national director of the National Association for Female Executives, it meant virtually no social life when she changed jobs about 10 years ago and moved to New York from Los Angeles. "I spent a tremendous amount of time with my son and foster daughters," she says. "I shaved things out of my life and enjoyed being alone. I hadn't done that since I was 10 years old."

"Good management involves reassessing company priorities just as often as family goals."

In my own life, setting priorities and saying no included the decision not to let my children have a dog. It seems like a small thing but the experience was instructive. My two daughters, now grown women, were about 6 and 7. I was a single mother stretched very thin between work and home in the wake of the breakup of my marriage. I figured I could not handle a dog. The disappointment for my daughters was acute, and there began an intensive lobbying campaign to overturn my decision: All the other kids in school have a dog. . . . Pets are good for children—they teach children responsibility and tenderness. . . . How can you be a good mother and not have a dog in the house? The facts were that I could not go to work, tend to the children and take on a dog, too. Family and job had priority.

But in a few years, the facts changed. The children

got older, my life settled down and one Saturday morning I brought home a golden cocker spaniel puppy.

The lesson here for managers is not just that you need to stick to primary goals in the face of opposition, but that priorities change. Good management involves reassessing company priorities just as often as family goals. It also involves reassessing your own strengths. Just because you can't take on an assignment right now doesn't mean you can't do it two years later.

Managing and Understanding

• Delegate. Another effective way to handle the Time Deficit—at work and at home—is knowing when and how to delegate authority. There is no way a human being can fulfill the stereotype of the dressed-for-success Super Mom and have it all. At least not all at once. But that doesn't mean that there are only two paths in the woods and that women have to make a lifetime choice between parenting in the home and super-starring at work. Maintaining ambitions as a family member and corporate executive demand redefining the work of both.

The management bonus here is that delegating tasks is a plus for staff or family members who in most cases thrive with more responsibility and authority. Before lawyer Gorelick had a baby at home, she tended to do all the work on a big case, leaving associates with a much lesser role. "Now I delegate more," she says. "I'm much more inclined to give the associate running room. It's better for me and everyone else. The associates are flourishing, the clients are happy and I'm happy."

• Listen. It's a cliché that women are inherently better than men at dealing with people—that they are more sensitive and intuitive about feelings. Obviously, that's not always the case. But there is something to be learned about understanding people and motivating them from the parenting experience. In "A Passion for Excellence," Tom Peters talks about MBWA—Management By Wandering Around—a style of management that encourages traditional top managers to step out of their white male ivory tower and get to know what employees are interested in, or afraid of, as a way to boost company productivity. "Leadership," he writes, "means vision, cheerleading, enthusiasm, love, trust, verve, passion, obsession, consistency. . . ."

"That's what women with families have done forever," says Patricia Harrison, 48, mother of three children and three stepchildren, co-owner of the E. Bruce Harrison Co. and president of the National Women's Economic Alliance. "We're looking at heightened communication skills."

• Motivate. "Management is finding the incentive that will motivate the individual," says Nancy Woodhull, 44, president of Gannett News Services and Gannett News Media. She is also the mother of an 8-year-old daughter. "Motivating a child can give you very good information for managing in the workplace. When a child can't talk, you've got to figure out what they're communicating to you," she says. "I have the ability to read feelings as well as facts. A male-dominated society discounts anything but facts and numbers. A lot more is communicated among human beings than facts and numbers."

• Reach out. A banker, who is 47 and the mother of two sons, points out that in juggling child-care arrangements, schooling, house repairs and community work, mothers deal with people of different education levels, economic status, ethnic and racial backgrounds. In the rarefied echelons of top management, there is often a white male sameness to the cast. The conventional old boys' network is defined by a narrow social class of certain schools, clubs, addresses, sports, vacations and, of course, a very high income.

"Unlike the old boy network, women get out of their class," says the banker. "They tend to relate better and more easily to individuals who are not like themselves. People perceive that and often will follow a woman's lead with appreciation."

• Be a team player. In management terms, families are teams. For most parents, the common good of the family is an established priority just the way the common good of an institution is a boss' priority. What mothers and good managers share is the sense of pride and satisfaction when the employee or child does well. "You're instinctively interested in staff development," the banker says. "You take pride and satisfaction in it. I think women are much less threatened by others who are building their career paths. They see themselves as part of a team, part of a family."

Be All That You Can Be

• Perform rather than please. This runs contrary to the popular myth that all women want to do is please people—especially the males in their life: fathers, teachers, husbands, lovers, sons, bosses and colleagues. This myth stems from fairy tale psychology that if you please Mr. Big, you get to wear the glass slipper.

But working mothers can't always be pleasing. In fact, the first thing that happens when a mother goes to work or becomes a parent is significant displeasure all around. Children are disappointed that Mom is not always at home (until they grow up and wish Mom would get off their backs); husbands are often disappointed with chaos at mealtime (until they get taken out to dinner); teachers are disappointed that you resigned from the PTA board (but you served last year); colleagues are disappointed because you don't schmooze as much (but you still produce); your friends are disappointed because they don't come to dinner as often (but they are all working, too, and don't go out much either); dentists are disappointed that you make appointments only at 7:30 in the

morning (but you still come and make the children go, as well); hairdressers are disappointed that you can only come at 7:30 at night (but my hairdresser is a mother, too, who works out of her home so it suits her just fine to work in the evenings).

In integrating work and family, parents with careers often encounter a storm of displeasure from people thay care most about—but the storm usually passes. In the process, you learn the hard way that getting the job done is more important than pleasing people. "Women learn determination and perseverance when the odds turn against you all over the place," says the banker. "You can't let the judgments of others affect what you're doing."

"A mother can't resign or find a new set of kids, so picking up the pieces and moving ahead becomes a habit."

• Handle crises. Taking care of children is a lesson in crisis management. A 3-year-old runs out in the street; a fifth grader is not back from school at 3 p.m. when you call; a teen-ager has a car accident. "Nothing on the job rivals the intensity of these moments," says Crisp.

Very quickly, mothers learn to take a factual as opposed to an emotional response to crises. As Sharon Kleiman-Altoff, 27, mother of an infant, a 2-year-old and a stepchild of 15, who is also vice president of BSC Litho, a commercial printing company in Harrisburg, Pa., explains: "The baby sitter calls and says the baby has a 102-degree fever. Instead of freaking out, I get all the facts: Is she throwing up? Does she have diarrhea? Then I decide whether to call the doctor and go home."

Another early lesson in parenting is how to survive your own mistakes. Holding a child back a grade may—or may not—be a wise decision, no matter how carefully you made it. A child gets burned by hot water while you're not watching. The little and big failures that are part of motherhood fuel the angst of am-I-a-good-mother? But failure also forces you to recognize the limits of what a parent—and manager—can do in the destiny of a family or a company.

Just as significant as failing is recovering from failure. Mothers do this all the time in families. A mother can't resign or find a new set of kids, so picking up the pieces and moving ahead becomes a habit. It's a habit every company manager needs when a major crisis erupts—a hostile takeover, bankruptcy, a costly product failure, unexpected death or injury of a staff member.

• Be patient. When parents read the fable of the tortoise and the hare to their children, they should apply the tale's lesson to the modern career race. With a life span now extended beyond 70 years, you don't do all your living in the first three or four decades.

For many working parents, the thirties are the arsenic decade when career is at a breakthrough point and then wham, here comes baby. For the first wave of working mothers who flooded the job market in the '60s and '70s, there were no rules on how to juggle competing demands. So any way you managed was okay. For the current generation of career couples with young children, the expectations of doing it all are higher, and the pressures to find the one right way—the one Super Track that integrates job with family—have fostered a sense of failure among those who feel that life is just not working out.

"Just when conventional fast-track men start burning out in their mid-forties and fifties, many working mothers get a second wind."

But as parents learn, growth and productivity do not go in a straight line but in rhythms. "You have to evaluate what your particular ambitions are and go after them—whether you're male or female. If family is an . . . overriding priority, then go for it," says Gannett's Woodhull. "Have the confidence and self-esteem that you're smart enough to make decisions."

Creating Role Models

In other words, there are many ways to manage during these years of raising children and building a reputation on the job. In the long run, it doesn't matter whether you work full time or part time, overtime or flextime; what matters is that you set your priorities and, well, manage.

There's a bonus here, too, when the children grow up and go on their way. Just when conventional fast-track men start burning out in their mid-forties and fifties, many working mothers get a second wind and enjoy a renaissance in their career.

In the process, they become role models for the next generation. As the daughter of Patricia Harrison told her mother when she went out to interview for a job: "Mom, what I did, I pretended I was you."

Abigail Trafford is health editor of The Washington Post.

Traditional Management Style Helps Executive Women

Monci Jo Williams

Reader, you have in your hands . . . a mirror. If you are a woman who works in a corporation, you may encounter yourself here—perhaps a middle manager, standing at the edge of a yawning gap that separates you from that next job in senior management. Or hurtling in midair across the abyss, in that terrifying make-or-break career opportunity, no net beneath you. Or standing on the other side—having arrived, safe, victorious, now a senior executive.

Men, you too may see yourselves reflected here. Not so long ago you had the corporate terrain all to yourselves. Then the women arrived, catapulted by some powerful but unnatural force called affirmative action. You may recognize the discomfort you felt, even resentment, as these invaders landed among you. And man or woman, you are very likely to see yourself in the executives described here, now struggling to define the common ground where they will compete and coexist.

Corporate Women

The managerial women now in line for top executive jobs are the first sizable group to compete head to head with men. Though feminists had once hoped women would "feminize" the corporation by making it more cognizant of family concerns, the opposite has in fact occurred. Successful female managers have taken on many of the values and life patterns of careerist men, who long have fixed an unblinking eye on the prize.

They are gutsy and gritty women in a man's world who refuse to let the feeling of being out of place become an obstacle. Most compete while retaining their femininity. Rather than try to change the corporation, they learn its rules, and they play by them. Anne Jardim, co-author with Margaret Hennig of *The Managerial Woman*, a pioneering study of women managers, believes that this is the only way for executives of either sex to get ahead. Says Jardim: "The issue for women today is not whether the world is fair. This is the way the world is. If you wish to be a part of it, live with it."

Women have gained a foothold within the corporation in a pindot of time. In 1987 they made up 45% of the work force and held 38% of the jobs classified by the Bureau of Labor Statistics as "nonfarm executive, administrative, and managerial," a rough proxy for middle management jobs. In 1972, the earliest year for which comparable figures are available, women were 39% of the work force but held only 20% of the managerial jobs. Women's advance into the highest ranks of American corporations, however, is less impressive. A survey by Korn/Ferry International, an executive search firm, found in 1986 that women held only about 2% of senior management jobs in America's largest companies.

Basic arithmetic provides some explanation. Corporations cull their senior executives from managers in their 40s and 50s with 20 or 25 years of work experience. Says Gerard Roche, chairman of Heidrick & Struggles, an executive search firm: "There are fast-trackers who get to the CEO's [Chief Executive Officer] suite in less time, but they are the exception." While that suggests that women as a group are advancing through the corporation on schedule, it may be too early to tell. Women trickled into the work force during the late 1960s, but the flood did not start until just about 15 years ago. Most female managers are still too young in years and training to have reached the upper echelons, but they are maturing into candidates for the senior jobs of the next two decades.

Even so, sociologists have noted a disturbing trend. Statistics are hard to come by, but James R. Houghton, the chief executive of Corning Glass Works, estimates that women and minority managers are dropping out of his company at roughly twice the rate of white males. Allen Neuharth, chairman of Gannett, believes that the progress of corporate women "has been much slower than it should be. That is primarily because there are still many white male executives who are reluctant to open the door to women."

> *"Successful women are realizing that they have joined a men's club where they must abide by the rules in order to win acceptance."*

Corning and such other FORTUNE 500 companies as Mobil and Colgate-Palmolive fret about the dropouts because demographic shifts are increasing the relative value of women managers. *Work Force 2000*, a book published in 1987 by the Hudson Institute, estimates that by the year 2000, native-born white males—long the corporation's main source of managerial and executive talent—will account for only 15% of the net increase in the work force, vs. 55% for native-born women. (The rest will be minority men and immigrants.) Says Felice N. Schwartz, president of Catalyst, a research group that advises corporations on women in management: "Companies will either have to dip deeper into the pool of less-qualified white males for future managers or attract, retain, and promote top women and minorities."

Keeping women on the job and promoting them in it is a problem that the women themselves and their employers are addressing. Successful women are realizing that they have joined a men's club where they must abide by the rules in order to win acceptance as members. An increasing number of men who run America's leading companies are concluding that their enterprises must adapt too. Says Corning's Houghton: "We must make the corporate environment more hospitable to women if they are to succeed."

Differences

Complicating the issue is the basic fact that men and women *are* different, a point the French have exclaimed on for centuries. Those differences become dramatically apparent, however, within the context of the male-dominated corporation. At their heart is biology: Women bear the children and—despite 20 years of "liberation"—they still raise them as well. Men have only one career to pursue single-mindedly; women must juggle two.

The other notable difference is cultural: Sheer competitiveness—*Get him! Go for it!*—is an attitude that is relatively new for women. Little girls may play on Little League teams in 1988, but most of the

women now competing in the corporation did not. They were raised by traditional moms to play with dolls, not baseballs.

When Mary Anne Dolan was editor of the *Los Angeles Herald Examiner* from 1981 to 1985, she made a point of hiring other women for the paper. Dolan hoped to create a happy family where colleagues supported each other in "honest conflict" rather than bruising competition, "making mincemeat of the male business model." She was disillusioned to discover, as she wrote in the *New York Times Magazine*, that the women she hired engaged in a "power grab." They wrote copious memos, they lobbied for their own projects, they gravitated to important senior managers—they adapted to the male environment.

The paradox for Dolan, who is now a syndicated columnist, and other ambitious women is that corporations—which are themselves engaged in a Darwinian struggle—can function only by encouraging competition in order to discover the fittest and ablest managers. Thus managers are encouraged to reward employees who are competitive. And ambitious women managers have leaped across the gulf that separates them from senior management by being good competitors.

Examples

Take Lucie J. Fjeldstad as an example. At 44 she is assistant general manager of finance and planning for the Personal Systems business of IBM and one of three women among the corporation's 46 board-approved vice presidents. Educated as an economist, she joined Big Blue as a systems analyst in 1968 and grabbed every opportunity to take demanding assignments that would advance her career. Like a checker jumping around a checkerboard hollering "King me!" Fjeldstad has hopped around the company developing and marketing hardware and software, as well as working on strategy, pricing, and budgeting. That experience, she believes, has given her "the kind of broad understanding needed to run a company." Could the company in question be IBM? Says Fjeldstad evenly: "You bet."

Blond, breezy Colombe Nicholas, 43, became president of the American subsidiary of Christian Dior in 1980. In eight years Nicholas has nearly doubled the number of U.S. licensees that manufacture Dior products, and her company's revenues have tripled to over $380 million.

Like most successful people, she worked herself up, step by tedious step. She began as a handkerchief and accessories buyer at Macy's where she realized that the hankies would never sell as they were displayed, in plastic rings that wrinkled the cloth. When the alterations department wanted to charge her 30 cents apiece to iron the 99-cent linens, she took them home and pressed them herself, standing over her ironing board on weekends and spraying each little white square with a Windex bottle filled with water. As a result, says Nicholas, ''we sold an awful lot of hankies,'' much to the astonished delight—and notice—of the boss. Nicholas outdid herself in every job and rose quickly through merchandising stints at Bloomingdale's and Bonwit Teller before joining Dior as its U.S. president.

When sociologists Hennig and Jardim studied managerial women in the 1970s, they found that the typical female manager tended to shy away from risk, viewing it as a chance to fail. The women who have fought their way up the corporate ladder, however, embrace it as an opportunity to strut their stuff and gain recognition. Claire Gargalli, 45, was an administrative vice president in the international department of Fidelity Bank in Philadelphia in 1974 when she was asked to go to New York for nine months to run the bank's international trading unit until the man who had been selected for the job could return from his post in London. Though annoyed that her bosses felt she was good enough to hold down the fort temporarily but not qualified to man the ramparts permanently, she decided ''it was an opportunity to prove what I could do at a distance, without headquarters looking over my shoulder.''

Her determination paid off. Nine months later, Gargalli returned to her job in Philadelphia when the man arrived from London to run the trading unit—and he was asked to report to her. Her stint in New York did not lead to immediate promotion, she says, ''but they did give me more money and my career progressed nicely from there.'' Gargalli is now CEO of Equibank, the $2.5 billion bank owned by Pittsburgh's Equimark Corp., and president and COO [Chief Operating Officer] of Equimark.

A Hostile Environment

Jumping into an environment that seems at times indifferent or hostile can be daunting to even the toughest competitor. Many of these women learned to compete and feel comfortable in a man's world because they grew up in one. IBM's Fjeldstad was raised on an alfalfa farm and cattle ranch owned by her parents in Cedarville, California, and spent much of her time helping her dad and a crew of 20 field hands run the ranch. ''My mother wanted a 5-foot ballerina,'' Fjeldstad says. ''She got a 5-foot 7-inch tomboy instead.''

Karen Horn, 44, is an athlete. The first and only woman to head one of the nation's 12 Federal Reserve banks, she is now the chief executive of Bank One Cleveland, a unit of Banc One Corp., the aggressive superregional bank. She has been an equestrienne since the age of 8 and specializes in dressage, a highly disciplined form of riding in which the rider guides the horse through intricate maneuvers with barely perceptible movements. The walls of her den are plastered with blue ribbons she

has won in competition.

Many of the successful women interviewed for this story had no brothers, and therefore had little competition for their fathers' attention. A lawyer and businessman, Dimitri Nicholas insisted that his daughter Colombe attend the University of Cincinnati law school, where she was one of three women graduates in the 116-member class of 1968. The principal preoccupation of her classmates was ogling the coeds and, to have something in common with the boys, Nicholas joined right in. Her classmates soon joshed that she was a discerning ''ankle man'' and began calling her ''Nick.''

''Many of these women learned to compete and feel comfortable in a man's world because they grew up in one.''

Jill Barad, 37, the executive vice president of design and product development at Mattel, has a sister but no brothers. She recalls, ''My father did not talk to us at the dinner table about growing up and getting married. It was 'Which one of you can finish the *New York Times* crossword puzzle first?' He used to say things like 'Never learn to type and you'll never be a secretary.' Without that encouragement from him, none of this [she spreads her arms to indicate her corner office] would have happened.''

Competitive vs. Macho

One way or another, these women were encouraged to be competitive, but they are careful never to out-macho the men. A surprising number of male search consultants and executives interviewed for this story held up Linda Wachner, 42, the tough, bottom-line driven chief executive of Warnaco, as a symbol of the right stuff in the wrong package. They give Wachner—one of the highest-ranking women in corporate America—high marks for her skill in managing Warnaco, but criticize her abrasiveness. But Wachner—who always worked for demanding, performance-oriented bosses and who can also be warm and charming—defends her style: ''Being effective is what matters,'' she says, adding, ''I'm not out to get corporate love. But I do have corporate respect.''

Still, many men who might admire or at least tolerate a harsh style in other men prefer that women tread the tightrope between toughness and femininity. Most of the successful women interviewed for this story manage this feat, and do not fit the current stereotype described by one male headhunter of ''men walking around in dresses.''

Though all of them with the exception of Wachner said they had encountered bias in their careers, none paid much attention to it. They succeed by being themselves. Carole St. Mark, 45, president of Pitney

Bowes's $400-million-a-year business supplies and services group, softened her approach after a painful episode early in her career. In 1970, when she was a recruiter for General Foods, the company sent her to a seminar on affirmative action that, as she puts it, "kind of elevated my consciousness."

Angered at instances of salary discrimination in her own short career—"We shouldn't have to pay you as much as a man because you have a husband who works," one boss told her—St. Mark returned from the seminar and wrote an inflammatory letter to General Foods' chief personnel executive. Fortunately, she carboned her boss, John Bulger. He came flying out of his office, a copy of St. Mark's missive in his hand. "Did this go out?" he demanded. "Get it back!" He then helped St. Mark rewrite the memo. "In a very calm way, he said he understood how I felt," she recalls. "But he also pointed out that the way I had stated my case would put people off."

Little Time for Families

As is true of fast-rising executive men, the responsibilities of corporate leadership leave the women little time for their families. Though St. Mark is now divorced, most of the women interviewed for this story are married and have children. Several delayed childbearing until after they had become senior executives. One woman who waited until she was in her late 30s to start her family—and then found that she could not conceive a child—reports that the fertility clinics are "jammed" with women like her. In a telling comment on the price women are paying for success, she shrugs, "You make a choice."

The demands of senior managerial jobs dictate that the executive mom must devote the bulk of her time to her work and squeeze her family into odd hours. In her role of bank chief executive, Karen Horn is also involved in a half dozen business committees and civic groups around the Cleveland area. She rises by 5:30 A.M. for aerobic exercises; by 6:15 A.M. she is in the kitchen flipping pancakes with her 6-year-old son. In September, Horn meets with her son's teacher to find out "key days on the school calendar" so she can plan her work around school plays and teacher-parent meetings. In her spare time she practices dressage with Ampersand, her thoroughbred; plays piano; and bakes bread to enter in the county fairs, often taking the blue ribbon there too. Says Horn: "I make the time by giving up sleep."

Successful women executives have discovered a basic truth long known to careerist men: It's easier to get ahead if you have a wife at home, or at least some reasonable facsimile thereof. These women buy from housekeepers, nurses, and caterers the cleaning, cooking, and child care services that wives once provided gratis. They also rely on husbands in

the "supportive" Phil Donahue or Alan Alda mold who become cheerleaders on the tough road to the top.

"Successful women executives have discovered a basic truth long known to careerist men: It's easier to get ahead if you have a wife at home."

In the eyes of the world, many of these wives are far more successful than their husbands; to traditional male executives such a reversal is often threatening. An executive search consultant refers to these men as "househusbands," but they are not. John Horn, for example, holds a Harvard MBA, has taught economics and marketing at the university level, and has worked as a consultant. When not managing the children's clothing store he owns or spending time with his wife and son, Horn plays piano in a classical trio and occasionally accompanies a soprano who sings lieder and operettas at benefits. He is less interested in a high-powered job, he says, than in living "the kind of life I want to lead."

Upward Mobility

The women profiled in this story have succeeded because they adopted some of the protective coloration of men. But what of the thousands of women who were not raised as athletes, who didn't grow up in a man's world, or whose fathers didn't treat them like substitute sons? In other words, most of the executive women who are trying to shinny up a very greasy pole. It turns out that help is coming from the unlikeliest of quarters—the corporation itself. As more and more companies confront the unusually high dropout rates of professional and managerial women—and the simmering frustrations of those who stay in the game—they are coming to the conclusion that part of the problem is the corporation itself.

Merck, Corning, Gannett, Capital Cities/ABC, and nearly 40 other companies have established programs designed to retain and promote women to executive jobs—by turning them into better-equipped, more confident competitors, and by encouraging male managers to accept them into the corporate ranks. The buzzword among human resources professionals and sympathetic chief executives is no longer affirmative action, but "upward mobility."

Though the push for upward mobility is more than affirmative action in drag, many of the basic issues are the same. Twenty years after corporations were strong-armed by the government to hire more women, most of the promoting is still being done by men. E. Martin Gibson, president of Corning's consumer and laboratory sciences group and the executive in charge of the company's upward mobility program, says that male managers in his company don't push qualified women for assignments and promotions. "Most successful men have had at least one sponsor who suggested them for a promotion, even if they were not aware of it," says Gibson, "but male mentors may be less likely to bet on women."

As a result, any chief executive who wants to make his corporation more hospitable to women managers must help change the attitudes or at least the behavior of men. And the consensus among a growing number of companies is that male managers need to be strongly encouraged to encourage female subordinates.

Several headhunters report that their clients tend to favor other men over equally qualified women for jobs. David Peasback, chief executive of Canny Bowen, a New York executive search firm, observes that women candidates are often rejected with the explanation, "We just wouldn't feel comfortable with a woman in that job." It would be easy to conclude that bias was the problem, but the truth is considerably more complex. People are most likely to behave out of habit, doing what is comfortable, and a surprising number of male executives are still uncomfortable with women colleagues and competitors.

Company Programs

For this reason, companies that want to promote more women start by helping them adapt to a male environment. They make sure distaff managers are fully qualified for promotion; that is, that the women know what the men know. Some send women managers to programs that sharpen their managerial and quantitative skills. Capital Cities/ABC discovered that many of its female managers are liberal arts graduates who need additional financial and management training. So the company enrolls promising candidates in the Smith Management Program at Smith College and the Program for Developing Managers in the Graduate School of Management at Simmons College, run by Margaret Hennig and Anne Jardim. These programs help build the women's confidence in themselves and—by no coincidence—the confidence of male managers in the women.

Some companies such as Corning, Gannett, and Merck take aim at the paycheck, tying managers' bonuses to their progress in reaching stated upward mobility goals. Merck, which has ranked as America's most admired corporation in *Fortune's* yearly survey for two years running, began to identify the most promising of its women in the mid-1970s. The company created a timetable to promote its top 10% of female managers, and it follows up on their progress. As a result, Merck has raised the proportion of women among its top 85 executives from 3.5% in 1983 to 11.8% in 1988.

After women managers began complaining to a Corning outplacement counselor about subtle forms of discrimination at headquarters, the company instituted a nine-point program to put women in 10% of the senior executive posts, 10% of the middle-management jobs, and 23% of the lower managerial and professional jobs by 1991. By 1988 those percentages were 3%, 3%, and 17%, respectively.

"Companies that want to promote more women start by helping them adapt to a male environment."

Many executives understandably dislike affirmative action and upward mobility quotas because they may favor unqualified over qualified candidates, a form of reverse discrimination that can undermine morale and productivity. Chairman Houghton, echoing the sentiments of many CEOs, says that he would prefer not to resort to numerical targets. "But," he says, "I haven't found anything else that works."

Quota-setting companies hope to make the best of this approach by ensuring that promising female managers get the experience they need to perform well when they are promoted. Martin Gibson stresses that Corning's plan has no magic solutions to lower the high dropout rate of corporate women; no one has. Not even gung-ho pro-woman chief executives like Houghton can reduce the commitment and time demanded by the corporation of its key executives. That is why women who are committed to careers, but take a leave of absence for a few years to raise children, will find their progress slowed.

Price of Equality

That fact of corporate life may seem unfair, but to paraphrase Anne Jardim, that is the way the world works. Success is a hungry god that demands constant sacrifice. Ambitious women who understand this are already on their way to the senior executive ranks in America's corporations, and are already reaping the rewards and satisfactions long enjoyed by their male counterparts. They are also making similar sacrifices. That is the price of success, and the price of equality.

Monci Jo Williams is an associate editor for Fortune, *a business magazine.*

Traditional Management Style Hinders Executive Women

Sherry Suib Cohen

Does a woman have to act like a man to make it in the corporation? Even in 1989, that's not a dumb question—especially given all the advice career women have gotten about changing their behavior to fit into the masculine, military-model corporate world.

This advice made a certain amount of sense in the 1970s, when women were first beginning to enter management ranks in significant numbers. Women managers were rare—women managers with track records virtually nonexistent. Establishing credibility did necessitate certain changes. Leave behind your feminine conditioning, career-oriented women were told, and adopt the language, the methods—and even the dress—of the men who run the show. It was the era of assertiveness training, talking about end runs and squeeze plays, giving up dresses in favor of the dress-for-success clone suit-with-bow tie. Armed with these tools and the determination to prove that a woman could do the job every bit as well as a man, a whole generation of female managers made their way into corporations across America.

The Situation Today

But how well did this advice to adopt the male mode serve those women—and how useful is it today?

Despite the spectacular performance of a few, women still are not as successful as they could be and deserve to be. Sex discrimination no doubt continues to be part of the problem, but it may not be the only roadblock. We have to recognize that there's something else at work, something that may be keeping women from achieving their full career potential.

Is it possible that some of our problems are even slightly related to the practice of women working as they think males would work? The traditional female upbringing, with its emphasis on nurturing, cooperation and empathy, has given many women a different approach to work and relationships than men have. Not all women are nurturers, of course, but many do bring these values with them into the corporation, only to feel that they don't belong there. Unlike Frank Sinatra, who does it his way, women are doing it "their" way—that is, the male way—and it may be handicapping their careers.

In masking their "noncorporate" feminine values, women pay a painfully high psychological—and perhaps professional—price.

Try working as a neutered person. Try working well and succeeding when everything you've learned about connection, warmth, friendship and empathy must be shed. In a tough world, where women are pulled apart by wishes to be themselves and still comply with what the workplace seems to demand, the only logical solution is to be everything that everyone wants you to be. Never mind that men never put such a burden on themselves.

It's not a question of blame. Who can chastise the pioneer feminists for dropping the traditional female values to adopt the male traits? In the early, turbulent days of change, it was necessary. But now it's time for reclamation. Until women stop hiding, defending or in some way contorting their nurturing traits, they will impede their own progress.

Some people don't agree.

Patricia McBroom, co-author of *The Third Sex*, for one. McBroom claims that the reality of today's corporate culture dictates that women will not gain the authority they seek unless they learn to emulate masculine job behavior. She does note that the "typical" corporate female executive in 1982 paid a heavy price for the masquerade. More than half of these typical corporate female executives were unmarried, and almost two-thirds were childless. By comparison, only 4 percent of the male executives

Sherry Suib Cohen, "Beyond Macho," *Working Women*, February 1989. Reprinted with permission.

were unmarried, and only 3 percent had no children.

The irony is apparent: Women senior executives give up an intimate family life to reach the top. And the men? The men give up nothing. It's time to reclaim our voices and our femininity. Unfortunately, even experts don't seem to recognize this.

Using Our Own Strengths

It might be wise for corporations to consider the study of managerial traits in a new context—the feminine context.

The feminine context combines firm direction with the genuine empowerment of others. It creates organizations that stir people to produce their best work because they feel good about the place where they work and about themselves. The skill to produce these feelings has real business value—as do other elements of the feminine power style.

The ability to manage change, for example. Robert H. Waterman, Jr., points out in his book *The Renewal Factor* that the only constant in today's business world is change. The most successful organizations are those that are "continually adapting their bureaucracies, strategies, systems, products and cultures to survive the shocks and prosper."

Women know best how to manage this kind of change—we with our instinct and ability to hold the changing family structure together and our age-old talent for smoothing over, accommodating and adapting. It is women who can best teach how to break bad habits, a prerequisite of managing change without breaking the backs of people.

How can we manage in the feminine context? We can do it with compassion, with curiosity and cooperation. We can do it through sharing the power and the glory. We can use what I call tender power, the power women always have used in their private lives. Now that we are an integral part of business, why should we discard what always has worked in order to adapt to an ethic of blind, unaffiliating, cutthroat competition?

"If you want to be a good manager . . . first be a good mother."

What, after all, have been the costs of this competition? We've all seen them: lagging productivity, a large turnover of the best people, political infighting and sabotage, workers who expect to be ignored and who expect to fail—and who do exactly that.

"If you want to be a good manager," says Lois Wyse, president of Wyse Advertising, "first be a good mother. All the things that a mother provides for her children—comfort, praise, scoldings, motivation, entertainment, teaching, punishment and

rewards—are what shape the basic behavior system for corporate interaction."

Mark H. McCormack, author of the best-selling *What They Don't Teach You at Harvard Business School*, suggests that ancient feminine tools like mollifying, empathizing and accommodating are sound business practices. "Acknowledge the other person's feelings," says McCormack. "This is the oldest psychological technique in the world and works just as well in negotiations as it does in any other form of human relations.

"Somehow," McCormack continues, "negotiating has been confused with machismo, as though the whole point is to outlast your opponent, to make him back down first." Slavish adherence to macho behavior doesn't work so well for men either.

When Tender Power Doesn't Work

Of course, some environments still seem to call for it. There always will be places where managing in the feminine context will be misunderstood or even seen as threatening.

"When you're part of a male macho situation," says Linda Kline, president of Kline-McKay, Inc., an executive-search and human-resources-consulting firm that serves many Fortune 500 companies, "there isn't a damn thing you can do but respond in kind if you want to go anywhere at all."

Though it's not useful to be a male clone, Kline stresses that too much disclosure of warmth can "scare men off. These men have been forced into molds that required them to cut all tenderness from their own psyches, so they're not going to countenance too many of these traits in women."

What should a woman in this environment do with her nurturing traits? In addition to outside outlets, like family and friends, the best policy is to "nurture down," to give your special care to those who are below you on the organization chart. "Empowering others makes them want to follow you anywhere!" says Linda Kline. "It will show in their work and will in turn make you—and your boss—look good."

Then, says Kline, if and when you get to be top dog you can do anything you please: "Women at the top rung of their business almost always use feminine traits. They are in the best position of all to nurture down and set precedents of cooperation and caring."

There are those who worry that nurturing down will simply be an invitation to underlings to usurp power. That fear is unfounded, says Barbara Tober, editor-in-chief of *Bride's* magazine and a woman who occupies a top rung in a powerful corporation. "When you give strength to others you strengthen yourself," she declares. "It's magical to discover that even when you think you're at the top of the ladder, there's always a new rung."

Tober doesn't discount the possibility of nurturing

up as well—a tactic some career women question. "I just feel as if I'm 'brown-nosing my teacher' whenever I'm tempted to show warmth or support or even give a constructive suggestion to my boss," says Nellie Gallant, an insurance salesperson from Topeka, Kansas.

"The feminine model of power can be powerful indeed."

It's important to move beyond this impulse, Tober stresses. "It was always 'her' against 'us,' and anyone who warmed up to 'her' was a traitor," Tober says of the student-teacher relationship. "Nothing could be more destructive to business and getting ahead than this particular philosophy.

"It is true," Tober continues, "that many executives are remarkably ungracious about compliments. But it is equally true that there are bosses out there who will melt from an honestly offered nice word.

"Try it. Go up to the boss, even if she's rushing down the hall, and say something like, 'I loved your last meeting, and I thought perhaps I could try this . . .' or write a note saying, 'I'm proud to work here, and I think I could do even more than I already do.'

"Not everyone will stop dead in her tracks to acknowledge you. And maybe you *will* be accused by peers of trying to butter up the higher-ups. So what? We're all so terrified of that possibility that we go full tilt in the opposite direction and ignore the teacher, ignore the boss and perpetuate a cold, hierarchical business atmosphere."

Both males and females on the top rungs have to be relentless about being role models of empathy if they want to put warmth and cooperation back into the corporation. But it is possible to make that change. And in a world where we all have to pull together, the feminine model of power can be powerful indeed. Following are five real-life examples.

Ellen Gordon

If any woman has found the secret of achieving business success without giving up the rewards of family, it is Ellen Gordon. She isn't thrilled about admitting that she has a management style different from that of her male counterparts, but she does.

"My style is more persuasive and insistent than loud and tough," says Gordon. "I'm certainly aggressive, but in a very quiet way. A woman who deals that way is less likely to be shut out from information that circulates along the communications network—information she absolutely needs. I think that women (and men too, for that matter) who don't continually try to prove their competence in loud and macho ways are much more persuasive than

tough guys are. I've always felt Don Juan probably wasn't much of a man, because of the way he was constantly compelled to prove it."

Gordon has managed the difficult task of moving up the corporate ladder while raising four children. "I once nursed my baby at the stock exchange," she recalls, "and thought they'd throw me out. They didn't know what to do with me. But I held my ground."

She is optimistic about the ability to have a family despite intense work demands. "It makes me sad," Gordon says, "to think that women who would want children under less pressured times will wake up one morning and be horrified that the opportunity is lost. You can always do most of it somehow, particularly if you have a nurturing partner and the courage to try alternative ways of being with your child. . . .

Lois Wyse

Lois Wyse's career as an advertising star began in 1963 when a jam company in search of a snappy and memorable slogan came to the firm she had started with her first husband. Wyse offered "With a name like Smucker's, it has to be good," and the rest is history. Winner of several advertising awards, including the coveted Clio, she is also the author of 50 fiction and nonfiction books.

Wyse, whose company is an established Madison Avenue firm, finds that businesswomen in general are more supportive of one another than their male counterparts are. Women still have to deal with that "old dumb thing of men who are critical of women," she points out. "When I told my partner what a great relationship I struck up with a woman who runs a huge company, his visceral response was 'Sure. You don't emasculate her.' Tired, tired thinking. If men would only put their dukes down, they wouldn't have to worry so much about being emasculated."

Wyse says she thinks of herself as a walking advertising layout. "The nicest, best-looking part of me is what I try to sell. If I choose to assume the role of tastemaker—and I have—I can't be a slob. Neither can I come on too strong or be inconsiderate of others. If these are female virtues—sure, I use them. Authenticity is what gives me my authority. I can't look and talk like ten years ago if I'm selling today's taste, and neither do I want to talk and look like someone I'm not—a male.

"Frankly," Wyse continues, "I think women who are all-woman are a lot less fearful about business than men are. They make decisions much more easily. That's because a man, for the most part, is his job and a woman is herself. I'm Susie, chairperson of the ABC Corporation, and I'm also Bob's mother, and I'm this and that—but a man, he's the chairman of ABC Corporation, and the minute he's not he falls apart and doesn't know who he is."

Despite her strong sense that a feminine power style works for her and for many other women, Wyse does not think it will work everywhere—yet. "Realistically, you are just not going to get to be the president of General Motors speaking in an authentic woman's voice," says Wyse, "because the men are just not going to let us in. We're going to run service businesses, we're going to run creative businesses, but in my lifetime I will not see a woman be chairman of General Motors unless some nice guy leaves her enough stock to assume control."

It will take more than one generation for women—and women's values—to achieve positions of such power. They must begin by establishing themselves in smaller businesses, says Wyse, and they must cool down. Cool down?

"Women do bring something special to the boardroom."

"Younger businesswomen are so confused about their roles today. There is too much hysteria, biological-clock nervousness, do-it-all frenzy," says Wyse. "They're told, 'If you're 40 you have a tenth of a chance to get married, and if you're 12 you can get married instantly'—that sort of thing. Their fathers are divorcing their mothers and marrying women 25 years younger. There's a lot of anger directed toward men and even anger directed toward other women who preceded them and who, many feel, have trapped them and told them a Superwoman story.

"We've got to go back to affirming those values we always held dear. In the end it will be the cool, unangry, caring heads who stay on the fast track to the very top. And it will happen."

Suzi Oppenheimer

State Senator Suzi Oppenheimer is a woman who has done it all—but in sequence—a life pattern attracting more and more assertive women. An MBA from Columbia Business School, Oppenheimer had four children in under seven years and moved to the suburbs just before the fourth—"because I'd always wanted to be involved in community life."

Soon Oppenheimer was not just involved but president—of the PTA, the League of Women Voters—the traditional women's roles. When her youngest was just entering elementary school, Oppenheimer decided to run for mayor of her small town—and won. After eight years she ran for election as state senator.

Now in her second term in the state senate, Oppenheimer has a strong sense of mission about her role. "I feel that it's up to women to humanize the political arena, since it doesn't seem to be a top priority for men," she says. "I've been an officer of the Legislative Women's Caucus, which comprises 24 women from the assembly and 5 from the senate. We have carved out for ourselves all issues pertaining to women and children. We champion, among other things, the search to find humane ways of caring for the elderly, the young, ourselves.

"We hear," states Oppenheimer, "that men are risk takers and that's how they succeed. It's the women who are risking everything, really. It is the core of women—its essence being humor, nurturing and the working that we do so well—that will give substance to the risks we take."

Oppenheimer has taken a few risks of her own—including that of showing emotion in public. She recalls a board hearing when she was mayor in which the community consensus was against permitting homes for the retarded in Mamaroneck. "I remember becoming quite emotional. I even cried—something I'm not crazy about seeing politicians do—as I made an impassioned appeal to allow these homes into our neighborhood." Community reaction to the plan and to Oppenheimer's position was very negative.

"I received so much angry mail the pundits thought I was finished. But you know what? The same community returned me to office with an even greater margin of victory than the year before.

"The public will forgive your not doing what they want if your principle is humane. I believe that. I believe America is yearning for niceness. Is it womanly? Or masculine? I don't know. It surely is human. I'm not such a paragon of virtue, but I want my four kids to live in a human environment."

Cathie Black

When Cathie Black became publisher of *USA Today* she promised to overcome the hesitation of nervous and reluctant advertisers about the new nationwide newspaper with "enthusiasm, optimism and water torture." Three years later, in 1987, advertising revenues topped $100 million, 35 percent higher than the preceding years.

Black has strong feelings about how vulnerable she lets herself appear. "I think it's fine to show emotion," she says, "but you cannot be emotional. It's a subtle but important difference. Perhaps more than men, women tend to display pride, happiness or sadness—but an emotional wreck in business is a disaster.

"I'll tell you a little secret," she says. "In situations where I feel most vulnerable, I'll turn to humor as a tool. I've observed many women do this, and they seem to do it somewhat better than men. Humor is a great gift because it is a great weapon. It deflects hostility, tension, anger."

Women do bring something special to the boardroom, Black believes. "It's clear that women can bring to the table a cooperative, participative management style," she says. "Women are used to consensus building, for example—the establishing of rapport.

"Years ago, I sat on a board for the first time, a volunteer-type thing. I went to a meeting and presented two or three new ideas—all brilliant, I thought—and one by one they were shot down. The next day a woman who'd been at the meeting called me up—I don't know if a man would have done it. It was such a splendid gesture.

"'Have you ever sat on a board before?' she asked. The answer, of course, was no. 'Well, we're going to have breakfast, and I'm going to tell you how to do it.' So we had breakfast, and she said to me, 'You know, what you've got to do is "seed" the board—plant an idea. Everyone likes to think he's the first to have heard something. So before you launch a new idea, make sure four or five people who will be present already know about it. Then they will support you.'

"She was a true friend, a cooperative agent."

Black does not, however, feel comfortable with the word "tender" as a way to characterize a good manager. "It gives a mixed message for business," she says. "Tender is sweet and caring, and it conjures up lovely things, but not strength and not confidence. The word 'tender' used with 'power'—it's, well, pink. I tend not to think of pink as powerful."

What does make for a powerful boss? "It's not necessarily a tough boss," Black says. "*Fortune* always lists the 'Ten Toughest Bosses in America.' I'd rather be thought of as one of the Ten Best Bosses, not the Ten Toughest—and believe me, there is a difference."

Black's list of the qualities the best bosses possess:
• Self-confidence;
• Ability to share glory;
• Caring personality;
• Decisive nature;
• Commitment to colleagues and projects;
• Enthusiastic skill;
• The courage to surround themselves with people more skilled than they are.

Harriet Richardson Michel

In her long career, which has included being president of the New York Urban League, Harriet Richardson Michel has found that her philosophy of what makes for effectiveness has evolved over time.

"Women managers did buy into wearing the pin-striped suits and an abrasive attitude for a long time," she says. "I've often found myself in a room being the only woman, the youngest, and the only black. Early on I learned to act macho to survive.

"For instance, I swear a good deal. I wanted, in professional situations, to be seen as 'one of the boys,' and if I was too feminine and if people had to protect their mouths around me, I wouldn't be admitted into the club—whatever club it was. So I

swore more and began to slap people on the back and be 'hail-fellow-well-met.'

"I was really caught in the middle. I'm 46 and young enough to have the '60s mentality that wants to cuss, because I was deeply affected and radically changed by the women's movement. At the same time, I have values that were formed partially by the traditional view of women, so a balance was hard to achieve."

> "Any woman who was a good homemaker, . . . who made sure she got her money's worth, was a great manager."

But balance is what is needed, Michel says. "However much we have either homogenized or sacrificed—I'm not sure which—we should retain or fight to regain the natural female instinct for management. We are surely more human in our management style. This is a very positive thing. If we can go into situations and bring the passional values that are unique to our gender, it only enriches the marketplace. When we're forced through a male sieve to deny these things, we inhibit a humane approach to getting people to work together.

"Any woman who was a good homemaker, who worried about getting money for the grocer and the dentist, who made sure she got her money's worth, was a great manager," says Michel. "Feminine was what she also was, and feminine is, of course, strong, firm and caring. Yet put this manager up against a man, interacting with him in business, and she's immediately seen as displaying negative behavior. It's so ironic. These good management traits are as connected to women as the humanizing traits are.

"Sure, doing things the tough-guy way may work better in the short term, because you scare the bejesus out of your workers," says Michel. "But in the longer term, they get so paranoid about their personal security that they lose their efficiency. The personal touch, whether it's feminine, masculine or human, allows workers to feel that their contribution within an enterprise is important.

"In the beginning, a woman displaying this personal touch may have it said about her, 'Well, that's just a woman thing.' In the end, if her productivity rises and the piece for which she's responsible runs well, no one can quarrel with her approach. We're talking bottom line here. It's up to women managers to show that women's traits are bottom-line effective."

Sherry Suib Cohen is the author of several books, including Tender Power.

"Research into the effects of infant day care clearly must proceed, and its implications may be great for parents and employers."

The Effects of Day Care: An Overview

Ellen Ruppel Shell

For many of us, the very notion of infant day care conjures up unpleasant, Dickensian images. Subjecting a baby to daily care by a surrogate so that its mother can work seems to go against the American grain. This may in part explain the explosive public reaction to reports of a review paper, "The 'Effects' of Infant Day Care Reconsidered," written by Jay Belsky, a developmental psychologist at Pennsylvania State University, for *Early Childhood Research Quarterly*. The paper reported that Belsky's research group, that of the psychiatrist Dr. Peter Barglow, of the University of Chicago Medical School, and others had shown that infants of twelve to thirteen months who have been subjected to more than twenty hours a week of nonmaternal care are at risk for future psychological and behavioral difficulties. Nonmaternal care includes day-care centers, family day care, and care in the infant's home by a babysitter or a relative.

Guilty Shudders

Newspaper reports about this finding sent shudders of guilt through millions of parents. The headlines have long since subsided, but what remains is the misguided impression that Belsky scientifically established what many of us secretly fear to be true: that mothers of infants who do not devote at least most of their time to child-rearing risk compromising their children.

The impression given by the report is quietly echoed by a handful of child-development experts. Dr. Eleanor Galenson, a prominent New York City child psychiatrist, told me that she has long considered full-time child care to be bad for infants and that Belsky's report simply confirmed what she saw in her practice every day—children whose psyches are seriously damaged in part because of a dearth of maternal attention. "Putting infants into full-time day care is a dangerous practice," she says. "Psychiatrists have been afraid to come out and tell the public this, but many of us certainly know it to be true." Another extremely influential authority on child care told me privately that despite public pronouncements to the contrary, he feels "in my guts" that infants are better off at home with their mothers.

Belsky's About-Face

Many psychologists and psychiatrists who specialize in the study of child-care issues, however, respond quite differently to Belsky's review. Many are outraged not only that Belsky would publish such a report but also that he would tout it on talk shows even before it was published. The announcement was particularly surprising coming from Belsky, who was well known for another review paper he wrote on infant care in a university-based day-care center in the late 1970s which concluded that "the total body of evidence . . . offers little support for the claim that day care disrupts the child's tie to his mother." Some accused Belsky of harboring a personal bias (his wife quit a professional position to raise their children) and of being publicity-hungry. Belsky dismisses such attacks as vulgar and inappropriate, but they illustrate the deeply felt nature of the debate. Probably no adult and surely no parent can claim to be completely unbiased when it comes to the question of how and with whom infants should spend their days. However, while it is not possible to settle the question, given the relative paucity of data on the effects of infant care, a closer examination of Belsky's arguments and the base on which he builds them does shed some light.

Belsky and others who study the effects of child care on children rely for their infant data mainly on the Strange Situation Test, which is simpler to perform than it is to interpret. The test was designed in 1964 by the child psychologist Mary Ainsworth, then at Johns Hopkins University, to measure a one-

Ellen Ruppel Shell, "Babes in Day Care," *The Atlantic Monthly*, August 1988. Reprinted with permission.

year-old's attachment to its mother. It involves seven three-minute episodes in which the child is left alone with its mother, then left with its mother and a stranger, and then left successively with the stranger, with the mother, alone, and with the stranger, until, finally, the mother returns for good. Observers judge how readily the baby can be calmed by its mother when stressed, and whether it avoids or resists her. Insecurely attached babies either avoid or actually push away their mothers, while securely attached babies seek their mothers out. Research that relied on the results of this test has demonstrated that infants raised at home who are insecurely attached to their mothers are at higher risk for future psychological problems than are securely attached infants.

In his review paper Belsky reported that his research group's study and three others all demonstrate that infants subjected routinely to more than twenty hours a week of nonmaternal care are more likely to show insecure attachment when tested. This insecure attachment is associated with "heightened aggressiveness, noncompliance, and withdrawal in the preschool and early school years." He concluded from this that extensive day care in the first year of life is itself a psychological risk factor. (Day care after a child's first year is not in contention here, and little is known about its effects.)

Precocious Independence

As Belsky himself concedes, however, the Strange Situation Test may well not be the best method for comparing children who experience day care with those who do not. The test was designed to measure infant attachment at a time when most children were raised at home. Belsky's critics point out that children in day care are subjected to what is in some respects a strange situation every day, when their mother or father leaves them in the care of someone else. Over weeks or months these children may very well get used to spending time with people other than their parents. Several psychologists have argued that infants in day care might simply have a precocious independence from their mothers—an independence that most normal children acquire over the next several years—and would not show stress if given the test. Belsky is troubled by this argument.

"I don't want to suggest that the Strange Situation Test is definitive—far from it," he says. "I have no qualms with the argument that we need new measures. But early research showed that day-care kids show the same level of stress due to separation as non-day-care kids [hence they are equally suitable to be tested for insecure attachment], and my critics completely ignore this data." Belsky's critics counter that such data as exist to support the notion that day-care and non-day-care infants experience equal

stress in the Strange Situation Test is at best inconclusive. Moreover, most of the research done in early-infant day care does not control for the quality of care an infant receives. And other than making an attempt at defining the economic class of an infant's parents, researchers barely consider its home environment. Yet parents who regularly use child care may differ in any number of ways from parents who keep their children at home, and these differences might be crucial to the interpretation of test results.

"Parents who regularly use child care may differ in any number of ways from parents who keep their children at home."

"The decision to place children in day care is correlated with many other variables, and this is absolutely the issue," says John Richters, a developmental psychologist and staff fellow at the National Institute of Mental Health, who wrote, with Carolyn Zahn-Waxler, a developmental psychologist at the NIMH, a rebuttal for *Early Childhood Research Quarterly* of Belsky's report. For example, parents who use full-time infant care may, on average, be under more financial strain than other parents; they may put more emphasis on their careers, or be less interested in domestic activities. "We have no idea what's involved here," Richters says. "Parents who use more than twenty hours of child care each week might share one or more other traits that would cause their infants to show a less secure attachment to Mother." Belsky acknowledges that studies have not yet taken these other variables into consideration, and says that doing so is "the current research agenda."

This methodological problem aside, the difference in maternal attachment Belsky reported between infants in day care and in home care, while significant, is not overwhelming. In the four studies Belsky reviewed, a total of 464 infants were tested. Of these, 41.5 percent of the infants in day care and 25.7 percent of infants cared for at home were insecurely attached. Alison Clarke-Stewart, a psychologist at the University of California at Irvine, who wrote a review of sixteen studies of infant care, found the differences to be somewhat smaller, with about 36 percent of infants in day care and 29 percent of infants cared for at home insecurely attached. (Studies in Europe, Israel, and Asia using the Strange Situation Test find about 35 percent of all infants in home care to be insecurely attached.) In all studies the majority of infants remained securely attached to their mothers regardless of their exposure to day care. There is no ignoring the question of why so many children in both groups test insecurely attached; so far there are no answers.

At any rate, Clarke-Stewart points out, even infants in day care who appear from test results to be insecurely attached are not necessarily at high risk of suffering from future psychological problems. "Belsky contends that child-care infants doubt Mom's availability and responsiveness, and that they develop a coping style to mask their anger," she says. "But this is an interpretation for which we have no empirical support. Children in infant day care have been observed to be normal. They are not emotionally disturbed." As for the implication of longitudinal studies showing later psychological problems for children raised at home who were categorized as insecurely attached on the Strange Situation Test, Clarke-Stewart and others say that day-care infants are by definition brought up differently from home-care infants, and that this difference in upbringing might well make it inappropriate to compare them directly.

"Comparing infants in child care with infants raised exclusively at home may not be very useful," says Kathleen McCartney, a psychologist at the University of New Hampshire who specializes in day-care issues. "We have no idea whether their differences, if any, are related to their day-care experience, their home experience, or other factors. Is child care a risk factor for infants? Well, it depends. What kind of child care are we talking about? What are the parents' motivations for using child care? What is the infant's personality? We do know that children in high-quality day-care centers do better than those in low-quality centers. We know that young children do better in small groups than in large ones. We know that children do better if their caretakers don't change frequently and are available, empathetic, and sensitive to the child's needs. But beyond that, there's not much that we can say that's backed by research."

A Risk Factor?

Belsky is dismayed by what he considers to be the misconstruction of his findings by political conservatives in anti-child-care arguments. "All I've said is that it's a risk factor," he says. "My purpose was not to castigate the very institution—just the institution as it exists today in this country."

In an as yet unpublished book chapter titled "Motherhood and Child Care," Kathleen McCartney and Deborah Philips, who is a psychologist at the University of Virginia, discuss the evolution of American child care in this country. They point out that our notion of motherhood is a romanticized social construct peculiar to contemporary Western culture, and they argue that American society's almost obsessive ambivalence about who should care for young children "reflects concerns that child care poses a threat to motherhood and the sanctity of the family." Child-care services, they write, "are rarely portrayed as supportive and complementary to the family, unless accompanied by paternalistic motives to rectify the effects of deprivation." It follows that the debate over whether children are slightly more or less attached to their mothers owing to early exposure to child care overlooks a much more fundamental conflict: the underlying uneasiness we as a nation feel with the very idea of infant care.

"Research should not distract us from the undisputed fact that bad care is never good for any child and good day care is all too hard to find."

Legislators and educators, who continue to question the role of infant care too, seem to put aside the reality that half of all infants today are regularly cared for by someone other than their parents, three quarters of them for more than twenty hours a week, and that that proportion is growing steadily. Research into the effects of infant day care clearly must proceed, and its implications may be great for parents and employers. But that research should not distract us from the undisputed fact that bad care is never good for any child and good day care is all too hard to find.

Ellen Ruppel Shell is a senior writer for the public television station WGBH-TV in Boston, Massachusetts.

"Any significant amount of nonparental care for very young children is unhealthy and to be avoided where possible."

Day Care Harms Children

Karl Zinsmeister

A rapidly growing share of America's children are being raised by hired workers, by substitute parents. Although most families still make arrangements so that either the mother or the father can stay home with very young children, every year more and more youngsters are handed over to caretakers, at a younger age, and for longer hours. While no one has any idea what the ultimate outcome of this giant experiment in proxy child-rearing will be, there is growing evidence that the long-term emotional, intellectual, and cultural effects will be unhappy.

The prospect of a "professionalization" of parenting has long disturbed some observers. One of the earliest cries of caution can be found in George Orwell's *1984*—which describes a future in which the state takes over the child-rearing functions of the family, with a resulting disappearance of close and intimate human bonds. Only among the ragged, sentimental, tradition-bound "proles" are children still raised by their parents. This primitive social practice makes proles hopelessly uncompetitive with the professional class that has come to rule the earth. It is also only among the proles that inefficient human traits such as loyalty, altruism, humor, and love continue to thrive.

The Last Barrier

Not everyone worries that public child-care will be harmful to society, however. In her pioneering book *A Lesser Life*, feminist Sylvia Ann Hewlett lodges a fierce protest against "the misguided notion that governments cannot and should not help provide a substitute for mother love and mother care," which she considers one of the last great barriers to economic and social advancement by American women.

"Brave New World: How Day Care Harms Children" by Karl Zinsmeister is excerpted from an article that appeared in the Spring 1988 issue of *Policy Review*, the magazine of The Heritage Foundation, 214 Massachusetts Avenue NE, Washington, DC 20002.

Yale psychologist Edward Zigler has called for turning the public schools into full-service institutions that would relieve the family of many of its traditional obligations. In the future, he urges, public schools should take over care of all children three and older, and play "a large role" in looking after infants as well. School buildings should open earlier and close much later, including on all vacations, so that parents who work could leave any child, from newborn on up, at the local school all day.

At present, day-care takes many forms, ranging from a live-in nanny to a large center located near a major highway exit. Nearly half of all mothers of preschool children are employed. As of the latest Census Bureau survey in the winter of 1984, their children were cared for as follows: 40 percent were tended by a relative, including the father; another 8 percent were taken care of by the mother while she worked, either at home or elsewhere; the rest were looked after by outsiders, with equal numbers in homes and in day-care centers.

The arrangement growing fastest is institutional care. Just from 1982 to 1984 the fraction of preschoolers in day-care centers went up 56 percent. By now, probably a third or more of all young children of working mothers are in centers, and the total is rising fast. Both advocates and opponents view group care in large, state-licensed and -regulated centers as the wave of the future.

This mass surrender of child-rearing responsibilities to nonrelatives—particularly to the state or other institutions—marks a profound change in human history. It represents the final victory of the industrial revolution: the industrialization of the family. From a purely economic point of view, having talented individuals leave the labor force for considerable blocks of time to rear their offspring is wasteful. The ultimate application of the principle of division of labor demands that the "job" of humanizing, acculturating, and morally educating our progeny be assigned to paid workers. If the results of industrialized child-rearing occasionally resemble Henry Ford's original assembly line, it should not be entirely unexpected.

Frighteningly Empty

In her book *A Mother's Work*, Deborah Fallows presents an unusual journalistic account of typical days in a wide variety of day-care centers. For more than a year and a half, she spent hundreds of hours in dozens of centers in Massachusetts, Texas, Maryland, and Washington, D.C. While Fallows discovered no abuse, little dirt, and adequate physical conditions in most centers, she nonetheless found the average child's experience to be frighteningly empty. This was a fairly typical visit:

> I settled into an inconspicuous corner of the room and began to watch the children. . . . Often, one child would attach himself to me—maybe going off for a few minutes but always coming back to say a few words . . . point to a shoe that needed tying . . . or show me his tummy.
>
> The teacher watching the children tried her hardest, ad-libbing her way from one activity to the next. She put on a record and started to dance. One little blond boy started dancing along with her. A few others joined the group. Five or six gathered by some swinging cabinet doors that formed the partition between the play area and the rest of the room. One little girl sat by herself, crying softly in the corner. The rest wandered around. . . .
>
> She gave up records then and tried reading a story. The same few eager dancers moved right in to listen, while the rest kept on swinging on the cabinet doors or aimlessly wandering. The little girl was still crying in her corner. After a short story, the teacher opened the large cabinet and pulled out some puppets. This immediately attracted the largest crowd of the morning. All but a few rushed right over to watch the show. But the brilliance of the idea dimmed after several moments. As her impromptu story line weakened, the toddlers drifted back to their swinging doors and wandering, shuffling their feet, chasing back and forth. . . .
>
> Here as at other centers I visited, you could almost feel the morning driving itself toward the grand finale—lunch.

In a day-care setting there is much rigidity and few surprises—standardization is the key to efficiency. There is even a uniform emotional environment, with scant room for individual expression; Fallows describes it as a constant "on" atmosphere, where charged hubbub leaves little time for children to muse, and where the pressure of numbers pushes even gentle and reserved children to react constantly.

Grace saying, coat donning, one-at-a-time hand washing—these become exhausting trials in depersonalization. Fallows gives wrenching descriptions of children referred to as "hey little girl," of activities that cater to the group average but leave the quiet children behind. She describes desperate notes sent in with youngsters by their parents pleading for extra attention and special comfort. There is much tedium, much bewilderment, many unconsoled tears, tired teachers doing what they can to get by, a lack of individualization in the best cases, no one really caring in the worst.

While day-care provided in homes tends to be less impersonal than the center-based variety, it also has many problems. For one, there will never be enough individuals willing to take children into their homes, or to go to other people's houses, to accommodate the demand. It is most often the elderly, young girls, and illegal immigrants who are willing to accept such a role today. And, although home-based care has the potential to be the healthiest kind for children, it is also where the most dangerous abuses occur. Conditions are extremely uneven and often difficult to assess. . . .

"There is . . . a lack of individualization in the best cases, no one really caring in the worst."

When, in the mid-1960s, demand for day-care began to rise, a quick flurry of studies suggested that nonparental care did children no harm and might actually be good for children in deprived environments. But, as the field began to mature and a younger generation of more agnostic investigators took over from the true believing pioneers, revisionist schools began to spring up.

Today, there are still relatively few good long-term studies, and research remains biased toward the best centers. As one professor puts it, "the lousy centers won't let a researcher near the place." And like so much social science investigation, there is always the risk of confusing the quantifiable with the significant. Much of what we need to know in this area is very hard to measure. But we are beginning to get some more sophisticated research. And it is no longer clear that day-care is good, or even neutral in its effects. Quite the contrary.

Belsky's About-Face

Child psychologist Jay Belsky of Pennsylvania State University, coauthor of the definitive review of the 1970s research, was viewed as one of the nation's leading defenders of full-time day-care for most of the last decade. Then in September, 1986, he published a landmark article in the bulletin of the National Center for Clinical Infant Programs that expressed serious concern over a "slow, steady trickle" of accumulating evidence that contradicted the view that day-care did not affect child development. The more recent studies, Belsky pointed out, looked more closely at such factors as age, gender, and amount of time spent separated from parents, and focused more on typical care-givers than earlier studies had. And they showed, Belsky said, two worrisome trends.

First, when babies less than one year old are placed in day-care, many of them develop weak and insecure bonds with their parents, bonds that are crucial to intellectual and emotional development. Weak parental bonds were found in poor children and upper-middle-class children in day-care, in children who attended good centers and bad centers, and in children who had high quality nanny-type care in their own home. "Whether it's a day-care center or a baby-sitter doesn't seem to matter," Belsky reports. Second, several different follow-up studies of children up to 10 years old show that among those with a record of early nonparental care there is more serious aggression—kicking, fighting—less cooperation, less tolerance of frustration, more misbehavior, and a pattern of social withdrawal. . . .

Warnings from the Experts

The recent research casting doubt on day-care is consistent with the views of pediatricians, child psychologists, and educational theorists. Among such child specialists, there has long been broad sentiment that any significant amount of nonparental care for very young children is unhealthy and to be avoided where possible. According to psychologist Claire Etaugh (a day-care advocate), of the 20 most influential child-care books published in the 1970s, only seven approve even grudgingly of both parents working while they have young children.

Penelope Leach, the British psychologist and author of perhaps the most influential child-raising handbook in America at the moment, *Your Baby and Child*, is a leading opponent of the trans-Atlantic trend toward mothers leaving their small children to go off to jobs. She speaks out regularly against group care for the very young, insisting that babies need the concentrated attention of their parents for at least two years. Someone caring for a child out of love will do a better job than someone doing it for pay, she argues, and social arrangements should aim to make full-time parenting easier.

Dr. Benjamin Spock has for years opposed infant day-care. Despite a good deal of backtracking in successive editions of *Baby and Child Care* in response to criticism from feminists, he still points out that "even at six months babies will become seriously depressed, losing their smile, their appetite, their interest in things and people, if the parent who has cared for them disappears. . . . Small children . . . may lose some of their capacity to love or trust deeply, as if it's too painful to be disappointed again and again." He adds, "It is stressful to children to have to cope with groups, with strangers, with people outside the family. That has emotional effects, and, if the deprivation of security is at all marked, it will have intellectual effects, too." Until a child is three, Spock now argues, he needs individualized care from the same person. Only in certain cases where the day-care fits that description fully can it substitute "pretty well" for parental care. . . .

"Someone caring for a child out of love will do a better job than someone doing it for pay."

The medical establishment, too, has voiced reservations about day-care. The American Medical Association warned in 1983 that day-care centers—where drooling, diapered, toy-sucking infants put their fingers in their mouths an average of every three minutes—were becoming dangerous sources of infections and disease. According to the Centers for Disease Control and other authorities day-care centers are responsible for rising levels of diarrhea, dysentery, giardiasis, epidemic jaundice, hepatitis A, infectious diseases of the inner ear, and cytomegalovirus (CMV) infection.

Many of the germs thus met would eventually have entered the child's system anyway at a later age. But given that a baby's immune system is not well developed until the third month, and not fully effective until about age two, early exposure can be risky. (And if CMV is brought home to a pregnant mother it can be very dangerous.) The standing recommendation of the American Academy of Pediatrics and the Centers for Disease Control is that all children under two should be cared for only with their siblings. When that is impossible, they recommend that no more than six children, from no more than three families, be grouped together. . . .

New Skills for Old Love

Day-care children, to be sure, often start out ahead of their home-raised peers in things like knowing the alphabet when they begin kindergarten. But does this amount to anything? Kids under age four, experts tell us, are not capable of much "achievement." In fact, formal education in those years can actually do harm, particularly if it is demanding or competitive. Many authorities now say that until a youngster is about five, little more than creative play ought to be solicited from him. . . .

Of course, love is not easily bought. Institutions can't hope to offer it. Only in a few rare instances can extraordinary individuals offer a child in day-care this love and personal attention he craves. A majority of caretakers are conscientious, and try to substitute for the missing parents, but fail anyway, for any number of reasons. One problem is sheer numbers—a single caretaker typically looks after from four to 15 children, depending on their age and the setting.

Another is continuity. Child developmentalists tell us that rapid shuffling of guardians is extremely traumatizing to a small child. (That is, until they learn not to get attached to any care-giver.) If a child is unable to develop secure adult attachments in the first three or four years, he can grow up simply not caring for anyone's approval and lacking any sense of accountability. Yet it is not uncommon for parents to change child-care providers two or three times a year (bad experience, sickness, child gets too old for that group, etc.). . . .

"Only in a few rare instances can extraordinary individuals offer a child in day-care this love and personal attention he craves."

But the deepest problem with paid child-rearing is that someone is being asked to do for money what very few of us are able to do for any reason other than love. Competent and safe baby-sitting, that is not so hard to hire. What will always be difficult is finding people who feel such affinity with the child that they will go out of their way to do the tiny precious things that make children thrive—giving a reason why rather than just saying no, rewarding a small triumph with a joyful expression, risking a tantrum to correct a small habit that could be overlooked but would be better resolved, showering unqualified devotion.

Ultimately, a child and a paid caretaker don't really share very much. Their relationship is commercial, temporary, practical. As one woman, a professional social worker who tended a friend's child in her home along with her own daughter, admitted to *Parenting* magazine, "I cuddle and kiss and hug this child, but the feeling is just not there." The experience of taking care of another woman's baby has convinced her that "nobody is going to provide my child with as much love as I can.". . .

Mothers Emulating Fathers

For years, one of the most cogent criticisms of American sex roles and economic arrangements has been the argument that many fathers get so wrapped up in earning and doing at the workplace that they become dehumanized, losing interest in the intimate joys of family life and failing to participate fairly in domestic responsibilities. Now it appears that workaholism and family dereliction have become equal opportunity diseases, striking mothers as much as fathers. At a recent conference on children, day-care campaigner Sylvia Hewlett told an anecdote about her efforts to convince the national accounting firm Arthur Andersen to institute a day-care policy because 40 percent of Andersen's professionals are women. Nearly all of these women, Hewlett pointed out, work "60 hours a week." It is essential, she argued, that programs be put into place so that after delivering their babies these hardworking employees can keep on in their jobs just as before. Apparently, Arthur Andersen's executives saw the business value in the plan and accepted her proposal. But what kind of human society are we becoming when we encourage new parents to hold "60-hour-a-week" jobs?

The quest for a humane child-rearing system is more than an engineering problem. It is a values problem. So long as we continue to debase parenting, only the debased will be willing to take it on. So long as people perversely want what they are not willing themselves to give, there can be no solution. The only way out of the natural shortage of good child-care is for every parent to devote more of his own time to his children, instead of hunting frantically, and quixotically, for more and better hired care. . . .

How To Stay at Home

We know that children benefit greatly—intellectually and emotionally—from parental attention. There is no "sound barrier," no moment when children suddenly stop needing their mothers and fathers. But at a minimum, experts counsel, we ought to aim for a situation where one or the other parent is devoting most of his time to the child until he is about three years old.

That could mean parents working at staggered intervals and alternating at child-care. More likely, it will lead to one parent working full-time and one working irregularly or not at all until the child enters part-time nursery school or kindergarten. (Which there is no reason to discourage. It appears that once they are about three, most children can benefit from the socialization of a few hours of nursery school two or three times a week.) The practice that many American parents already follow—incrementally increasing their participation in the paid labor force as the youngest child begins attending some school—seems to be sound. Parents and children both can benefit from an increase in family income. If parents find work stimulating, their satisfaction and confidence will overflow into the family. But these benefits disappear if work begins to cut into the child's time at home. . . .

For reasons most parents already sense, paid day-care ought to be a distinct second choice, and group day-care in institutions a last alternative.

Karl Zinsmeister is an adjunct research associate at the American Enterprise Institute in Washington, DC.

Day Care Does Not Harm Children

Susan Faludi

In 1988 I was sitting in a classroom at Stanford University's Business School, listening to a seminar on parenting. It was one of three postfeminist-minded seminars the campus women's group was sponsoring on motherhood. (The session the following week was entitled "The Biological Clock.") On the panel, five women and one man took turns explaining how they managed full-time careers and children. They were actually quite successful at balancing work and family—even, god forbid, happy to be doing both.

But the students would have none of it.

Don't you worry about your kids being "emotionally scarred"? they interrogated the panel. Wasn't child care "damaging"? Wouldn't it be better for the kids if you stayed home? At the end of the session, one of the students, a new mother, approached the panel, her brow furrowed. "Is there any data to show that it's bad for kids to be in day care?" "Actually," one of the speakers said, "just the opposite; there are many advantages to day care. . . ." But before she could finish her sentence, the young mother interrupted: "I know all that. But I just keep thinking that it can't be, you know, healthy."

Day-Care Bashing

The young mother surely could have gotten that impression by reading the popular press over the last few years. A few sample headlines from well-read magazines: "'Mommy, Don't Leave Me Here!': The Day Care Parents Don't See." "When Child Care Becomes Child Molesting: It Happens More Often Than Parents Like to Think." "Creeping Child Care . . . Creepy." Day-care bashing seems to be a sanctioned sport in the media, even in these supposedly enlightened times when the working mother is accepted, albeit begrudgingly, as a

"reality." . . . To most legislators day care remains, like welfare payments or prison construction, a necessary evil. Even U.S. Senator Christopher Dodd—sponsor of the most generous legislative package, the ABC child-care bill—hastened to mitigate his defense of child care in a letter he wrote in 1988 to the *New York Times*: "No one is debating whether parents who can afford to stay home provide the best care for their babies; of course they do."

As day-care centers have proliferated in the last decade, politicians—and their constituents—have been forced to acknowledge their place in the late 20th-century social landscape. But the explosive growth of the child-care industry has not stilled private apprehension toward the institution. If anything, as the number of day-care centers rises, so do suspicions. The press has picked up on the signals emanating from an American public uneasy about day care, and has done its part to broadcast and amplify them. Day-care centers, we are warned repeatedly in the media, are magnets for disease and deviants. Various "experts" are summoned to prepare us for the worst. The *New York Times* quotes a typical spokesman of doom, who advises anxious parents: "Pedophiles are naturally drawn to jobs where they have close contact with children." *Newsweek* demands shrilly in a cover headline: "Who's Minding the Children?" and focuses on the face of a frightened-looking, saucer-eyed child sucking his thumb. Two weeks before, the same magazine had warned of "an epidemic of child abuse" in day care; this later issue showcases a Good Mother who junked her career to be home with baby: "I had to admit I couldn't do everything," she states in a photo caption, an admission that clearly earns an approving nod from the *Newsweek* editors.

It was with some puzzlement, then, that I stumbled across a story buried near the classifieds in

Susan Faludi, "Are the Kids Alright?" *Mother Jones*, November 1988. Reprinted with permission.

the *New York Times* one morning soon after the Stanford seminar, reporting the findings of the most comprehensive study ever conducted on sexual abuse in day-care centers. The three-year, $200,000 study by the University of New Hampshire's Family Research Laboratory found that if there is an "epidemic" of child abuse, it's in the home—where children are almost twice as likely to be molested as in day care. And, ironically, the researchers found that children were *least* likely to be sexually abused in day-care centers located in high-crime, low-income neighborhoods (there tends to be more supervision in these centers). Despite frightening stories in the media, the researchers concluded, there is no indication of some special high risk to children in day care.

The Family Research Laboratory scoured the national statistics on sexual abuse; it came up with 1,639 cases of children who had been sexually abused in day-care centers—out of the seven million children in day care nationwide. By contrast, out of 21.3 million children under age six, it counted 76,000 who had been molested at home. The lab study also found that physical abuse is far more rampant in the privacy of the home than in day care. And when the parents are the perpetrators—as Linda Meyer Williams, the study's project director, points out—the consequences are graver. "Intrafamilial abuse tends to be of longer duration, more serious, and more traumatic to the child because of the question of trust," Williams says. "There is some evidence that the closer the relationship, the greater the impact."

Unwarranted Hysteria

Although many of the celebrated tales of day-care workers molesting children since 1983 have turned out to be tall tales, we continue to believe their message. "The consequences of all the negative play in the press about the McMartin case were really quite dramatic," says Abby Cohen, managing attorney of the Child Care Law Center, referring to the 1984 sex-abuse scandal at the McMartin Pre-School in Manhattan Beach, California. "Because, unfortunately, up until then there hadn't been very much play about child care, period. So it was terribly detrimental that the first real wide attention to it was in such a negative light." Seven other day-care centers near Manhattan Beach were forced to shut down in the ensuing hysteria, though police found evidence to support parental allegations of abuse in only one center. At another center in the area, the owner was plagued by telephone death threats, her home vandalized; upon investigation, the charges against her center proved groundless.

The bad press has been especially hard on male day-care workers who, after daring to cross sex-stereotype lines to enter a "female" job, now find themselves pegged as perverts. Since 1984, male day-care workers have quit the field in droves. In an attempt to counteract the flight, Bernie Mueller, assistant director of child-care services at UCLA, started running monthly support groups for his beleaguered male colleagues. "We feel like suspects much of the time," he says. Mueller, who has worked in day care for 20 years, felt that way himself after one of the mothers at his center implied that someone on the staff had been the cause of her daughter's rash. It turned out that the culprit was Mr. Bubble; the little girl was allergic to the soap.

"What should be most curious to anyone reviewing the voluminous research literature on day care . . . is the chasm between what the studies find and what people choose to believe."

The findings of the Family Research Laboratory probably won't help to alter appreciably the internalized anxiety over day care. What should be most curious to anyone reviewing the voluminous research literature on day care to date is the chasm between what the studies find and what people choose to believe. Much of the research indicates that if day care has any long-term effect on children at all, it's made them somewhat more social, experimental, self-assured, cooperative, creative. At the University of California at Irvine, Alison Clarke-Stewart, professor of social ecology, found that the social and intellectual development of children in day care was six to nine months ahead of children who stayed home. In these days of the one-child household, youthful companionship and socialization are more commonly found in day care than at home.

A friend of mine discovered this advantage without the aid of academic research after sending her only son Ben, 2½, to day care. He started to miss the action on the weekends. "One weekend my husband and I were just lying around the house, not doing much," my friend said, "and Ben wanted to know if we could drop him off at day care. He seems to think there's an ongoing party over there." Since Ben started day care, his vocabulary has expanded and his social skills have improved.

One morning I accompanied Ben to day care, and heard a similar story from the other parents. This, by the way, is no Better Baby Institute for the elite, either: a $45-a-week, no-frills, home-based center in a working-class neighborhood of San Francisco, the floor is cluttered with worn tricycles, a couple of Big Wheels, simple wood blocks. The day-care provider is a retired nursery school teacher with no advanced degrees in child development.

"To tell you the truth, it was much more difficult for me than it was for him," one mother, Mary Dettle, said as she dropped off her son Lance. "Lance loves coming here. When I tell him it's time for day care, he grabs his coat and runs to the car. When he first started coming here at eight months, he was a little behind developmentally. Within a few weeks, he'd learned to crawl; he tried to stand. All of a sudden he was verbalizing."

"Well, David has gone from being kind of a problem to doing extremely well," Novella Smith, another mother, said. "He was whiny around the house, and that pretty much went away after he came here. He learned to walk real fast, I think to keep up with the other kids. He's very social now, not at all intimidated by new situations. And he's become shockingly verbal."

The research on day care points to other bonuses, too. Day-care kids tend to have a more progressive view of sex roles. Canadian researchers Delores Gold and David Andres found that the girls they interviewed in day care believed that housework and child care should be evenly divided; the girls raised at home still believed these tasks are women's work. We are reminded constantly in the press that children in day care turn out to be too "aggressive." But researchers point out that what is being billed as aggression could as easily be labeled assertiveness, not at all a bad quality in a child.

For children of poverty, day care may be their ticket out of the ghetto. The studies find that the futures of low-income kids brighten immeasurably after a couple of years in day care. The Perry Pre-School Project of Ypsilanti, Michigan, followed 123 poor black children for 20 years. The children who spent one to two years in preschool day care, the researchers found, stayed in school longer, were not as prone to teenage pregnancy and crime, and improved their earning prospects significantly. A study of 750 Harlem children by New York University came up with similar results: the children enrolled in preschool were far more likely to get jobs and pursue education beyond high school.

"Researchers point out that what is being billed as aggression could as easily be labeled assertiveness."

It is this bias that makes our day-care terrors so intractable. It is what prompted the Stanford business student to say, despite the evidence, that day care still "can't be, you know, healthy." If the feeling comes from the gut, if it is an internalized, strictly personal belief, then its truth must be of a higher order, unassailable by any number of studies.

But what the business student and many of her generation fail to see is how our seemingly personal perceptions of day care are not so personal after all; how they have been shaped by forces that have little to do with gut instinct. Our opinions have been hammered by eight years of relentless anti-day-care/anti-working-mother rhetoric from the Reagan administration. And, as if to back up its assertion that day care will stunt our children, the federal government has gone out of its way to make this a self-fulfilling prophecy by cutting day-care subsidies and dispensing with efforts to regulate and enforce quality-care standards in day care. (Regulating day care does have an effect: according to the Children's Defense Fund, child-care centers with lower standards and less parental monitoring are five times as likely to generate complaints. In New York City, of the 18 substantiated cases of child abuse at day-care centers, 17 cases occurred at unlicensed facilities.)

The Healthy Way

Politics is not the only external influence; cultural forces are at work here, too. We suffer a compulsion to replicate our childhoods, no matter how unpleasant those early years might have been. If our mothers stayed home, that must be the "healthy" way. What we forget is that it's only been since the 1940s that public opinion has so insistently endorsed the 24-hour-mom concept. The Victorians may have kept their women at home, but not for the sake of the children. "An educated woman," writer Emily Davies advised mothers in the 1870s, "blessed with good servants, as good mistresses generally are, finds an hour a day amply sufficient for her domestic duties." An early version of quality time.

The paranoia may ease once the younger generation reaches adulthood; they are not freighted with the same cultural assumptions about child care as those weaned in the 1950s. I brought up the matter of child rearing to teenagers at Lowell High School in San Francisco. They all seemed to favor day care more than their parents do. How come? "Well," one 17-year-old girl reasoned, in what turned out to be a typical response, "I went to day care when I was little and I had a really good time."

There are studies, too, to counteract the other favorite bugaboos. The specter of illness, for example: children are prone to disease at first, but once they build up immunities, they tend to get sick less often. There's a slight increase in the number of colds, but even kids at home rack up an impressive six to eight colds a year. And then there's the threat to "bonding": children often form affectionate attachments with day-care workers, but in at least a dozen studies, that attachment was found to in no way diminish the emotional bonds between mother and child.

Presented with the evidence, some day-care critics will concede that preschool may have a negligible effect on toddlers, but then they move quickly to the matter of infants. So three-year-olds may survive day care, they say, but newborns will suffer permanent damage. Their evidence comes from two sources. The first is a collection of studies conducted in the 1940s, '50s, and '60s in France, England, and West Germany. These studies concluded that infants who were taken from their mothers had tendencies later toward juvenile delinquency and mental illness. But there's a slight problem in relying on these findings: the studies were all looking at infants in orphanages and hospital institutions, not day-care centers. The West German study actually involved monkeys, not human babies, whose mothers were replaced by a wire-mesh dummy.

Biases Against Day Care

The other source frequently quoted is the much-celebrated turnabout by the Pennsylvania State University psychologist Jay Belsky, a one-time leading supporter of day care. In 1982, Belsky had reviewed the child-development literature and concluded that there were few if any significant differences between children raised at home or in day care. Then, in the September 1986 issue of the child-care newsletter *Zero to Three*, day-care champion Belsky announced that he had changed his mind: children whose mothers work more than 20 hours a week in their first year, he said, are at "risk" for developing an "insecure" attachment to their mothers. Belsky's pronouncement provided grist for the anti-day-care mill—and was widely reported. What did not receive as wide an airing, however, is the evidence Belsky cited to support his change of heart. Two of the studies he used flatly contradict each other: in one of them, the study's panel of judges found the infants in day care to be more insecure; in the other the panel found just the opposite. The difference in results was traced to the judges' own bias against day care. In the study where the judges were not told ahead of time which babies were in day care and which were raised at home, the judges said the children's behavior was indistinguishable. In the study where they did know ahead of time which babies were in day care, they concluded that the day-care children were more insecure.

Susan Faludi is a staff writer for the Sunday magazine section of the San Jose, California, Mercury News.

The Government's Role in Child Care Should Be Expanded

Carol Polsgrove

I had my first lesson in the economics of child care when my daughter was five months old and I was almost ready to go back to work half-time. She seemed so very little to me still—oh, big and sturdy as babies go, but so small and uncertain about life. Whom would I find to trust her with, four hours a day, five days a week?

I tried leaving her a couple of times with a woman who took care of a friend's baby, plus several toddlers, but I was depressed by the small, dim house and the grime ground deep in the carpets and furniture. I could not imagine how my child, who seemed to take 150 per cent of my time and energy, could be happy sharing a care-giver's attention with another baby and two or three toddlers.

And so, one Saturday morning, off I went to Bananas, our renowned Oakland child-care referral center, for a seminar on looking for child care. Not surprisingly, the seminar was popular; half of all mothers with preschool children now work, including half of all married mothers with children under two. About thirty parents were there at Bananas that morning—mostly mothers, with a few fathers, including one by himself with his infant.

We sat on folding chairs while our babies lay or crawled on quilts on the floor in front of us or sat on our laps. We began by going around the half-circle, saying our names and reasons for being there.

Suddenly the solution to my problem seemed simple. Sitting next to me was a mother with a baby the same age as mine. And she wanted to delay going back to work a while longer by taking care of someone else's child along with her own. She was, besides, a registered nurse and lived in my neighborhood.

Over the next couple of weeks, we strolled our babies to the lakeside park and visited each other's

apartments. I was delighted each time I saw her: She was warm, caring, intelligent, and versed in contemporary wisdom on child-rearing.

She had not yet determined the fee she would charge, and I held my breath. She called Bananas and was told that $3.50 an hour was really the most she could expect to ask, considering the market.

Economically, this was not going to be a great deal for either of us. She, accustomed to a nurse's salary, could scarcely have felt good about her new income as a child-care worker. She would be joining an occupational group ranked in the lowest 10 per cent of all wage earners, even though its members have a higher-than-average education level. For my part, I would be paying $14 a day for the four hours' work—$280 a month out of take-home pay of $1,000.

Costs out of Reach

I was surprised by the cost, although I shouldn't have been. The evidence was there: Full-time child care averages $3,000 a year nationwide. In California, infant-care costs average about $4,200 in centers and $3,300 in family day care—the term used for a woman caring for children in her own home.

As the *AFL-CIO News* has put it bluntly, "Child care costs are out of reach of all but the most affluent American couples." Full-time wage and salary workers earned a median income of $19,396 in 1987, the *News* reported. Child care for two children would use up about 30 per cent of that. The numbers are even worse for women alone: Women's median income was $13,008 in 1987, and child-care costs would consume almost one-fourth of that for each child. A minimum-wage worker with two children would spend almost all her income on child care—a no-win proposition.

As things turned out, my nurse friend did not take care of my child, not because the economics weren't right—although this may have been an unvoiced consideration—but because she tried taking care of both babies and began to doubt that she could care for them safely. They had reached the age when they put everything in their mouths: decaying crumbs, pennies, thumbtacks. Left on a sofa, they rolled off. Left alone in a room, they pulled floor lamps down on their heads or strangled themselves with the cords. Making the room child-proof was no guarantee of safety; they had to be watched.

Safety Issues

Considering her misgivings, I could not—cannot—imagine how so many licensed family-day-care workers cope with four infants. Aside from the issue of safety, how can one person provide the individual attention that four babies need, hour after hour after hour, for eight to ten hours?

Children under one can do nothing at all for themselves, nor can they say what it is that needs doing. The adults taking care of them have to figure it out: Are they crying because they are thirsty or hungry? Or because they need a fresh diaper? Or are they simply bored—tired of lying alone in a crib while their care-giver changes the diapers of three other babies?

Suppose that one well-organized person can maintain reasonable standards of safety and health, which is not easy. What about standards for mental and emotional growth? The juries of experts are still out on that question, but experts and parents alike are perceptibly more nervous about child care for the very young, those under a year old, unless the care-giver has the chance to develop a real parental relationship with the child.

Many care-givers do not have that chance; they can't afford it. If all a parent can pay is $2 an hour, then four infants bring in only $8 an hour, before expenses. No wonder, then, that a certified family-day-care worker will try to care for at least four infants—a number allowed by most states. Or she may expand her operation to a more manageable mix of toddlers and infants—say twelve in all—if she can use a relative or teen-ager as an aide.

"An estimated nine million children under six are cared for, at least part of the day, by someone other than their mothers."

Many, many day-care providers are not certified by the state and they take in all the children they can. Jessica McClure, the Texas toddler who fell down a drill-hole, was one of nine small children being cared for by one woman, unlicensed to provide child care. An estimated nine million children under six are cared for, at least part of the day, by someone other than their mothers, and there are only two to three million licensed slots.

I was lucky: I had retired parents to fall back on. They moved from Kentucky to California for a three-month stay, in a separate apartment. They did a superb job, and my daughter thrived. There was a cost, of course, which they paid—the cost of two round-trip plane fares and apartment rental. For them, it was an expensive solution.

When they left, and with their financial help, I reduced my teaching load to one-quarter time and, for child care, exchanged a half-day a week with a friend—another single mother—and paid a college student for the other half-day. Such repeated reshuffling of child-care arrangements seems common, at least among people I know. With so much of child care dependent on relatives, neighbors, and part-time or temporary workers who are always looking for something better—and with children themselves outgrowing one situation and needing another—no child-care solution seems more than provisional.

Summer came, and my daughter was fifteen months old, well past the age when many children are cared for in groups other than their families, so I thought she might be ready to give it a try. The friends who had steered me first to their family-day-care provider—the woman with the dim home—had moved on when she went out of business. Their toddler now stayed at a parents' cooperative, not licensed but staffed with part-time child-care workers. The staffers were paid a relatively handsome $7 an hour, plus health benefits, and parents took regular turns helping out.

Economics of Child Care

I signed my toddler up there. I was about to learn my second lesson in the economics of child care.

This little co-op, home away from home for eight children under two, was not a fancy place. It was housed in what, in Berkeley, is called a cottage; back in Kentucky, we would call it a shack. And even that shack was about to be taken away. The landlord, claiming other plans for the property, wanted the co-op out. Frantically, the parents and staff searched the area for a substitute the co-op could afford and a landlord willing to rent.

The best we could find was the downstairs of a large two-story house, next to a vacant lot in Oakland's vast west-side poverty district—what we would once have called a ghetto. Several parents demurred; they would not feel safe coming to pick up their children after dark. Finally, the group settled into a month-to-month lease in an even smaller cottage across the street from the old one, the best choice available. The deal closed with the understanding that the landlord could evict at any moment and use the property in another way.

By this point, summer was over, and my daughter, never happy in the group setting, cared for by a stream of strange people, was comfortably installed again with her generous grandparents, who had moved back to California to take care of her while I taught full-time.

But my experience with the co-op reinforced that first economics lesson with my nurse friend: The amount that good child care costs far exceeds the amount that most parents, even middle-class parents, can pay. If the best that we lawyers and teachers could offer these small children of ours was a rotating cast of care-givers in a shack in a ghetto, what can restaurant workers and sales clerks hope to find?

In fact, many low-income families rely for infant care on relatives, as I did, whether or not those relatives are, as mine were, particularly willing or financially, physically, and emotionally able. Nearly half of all working mothers of children under five depend on relatives, including fathers, for child care.

If relatives are not available and parents cannot afford even low-quality family day care, they arrange their work schedules so that older siblings—not even that much older—can babysit. Or they leave their babies alone at night, when they are presumably sleeping, with someone in a neighboring apartment listening out for them.

What we have, plainly, is a two-tier system of child care, with low-income families excluded from the market of adequate care.

"What we have, plainly, is a two-tier system of child care, with low-income families excluded from the market of adequate care."

A few low-income families are able to get subsidized care, but very few, and 90 per cent of those are single mothers. Federal funds for direct day-care subsidies have dropped under the Reagan Administration. Funds allotted under Title XX of the Social Security Act, the chief source of Federal subsidies to low-income families, are now half what they were ten years ago.

Left to their own devices, the states have met a mere fraction of the need. The state of Georgia, for example, serves only 8,000 of the 76,000 eligible for subsidies. Nearly 30,000 children in Florida are on the waiting list for subsidized care. Twenty-two states are actually helping fewer children than they were six years ago.

"By the mid-1980s, the only children who were assured of access to a subsidized place in care were children in need of protection against neglect and abuse," write Alfred J. Kahn and Sheila B. Kamerman in their book, *Child Care: Facing Hard Choices.* "Indeed, in several states, there was a basis for suspicion that this group had grown, in part,

because some parents were prepared to label themselves neglectful or potentially abusive to qualify for decent affordable care."

Even in California, the biggest state spender on child care, the demand for infant-care subsidies far exceeds the supply. Bananas, one of the private agencies channeling state subsidies to providers, has 100 slots for children under two-and-a-half. Because the program is limited to such a short time span, there is a fair amount of turnover. And still the waiting list numbers 600.

Difficult Choices

If the economics of adequate child care dictate that most of us have a hard time affording it, what are we working parents to do?

As individuals, we find ourselves making difficult choices: not to have a second child, not to buy a house, not to work; to live in an unsafe neighborhood, to have an abortion, to suppress the fear that our children are unsafe and neglected.

As a society, we surely cannot let this situation go on. It is tolerable neither for parents nor for children nor for child-care workers.

Business also has a stake in this issue. In *American Demographics*, economists David E. Bloom and Todd P. Steen note the signs that the supply of new workers willing to take low-paying, entry-level jobs is dwindling. More available, affordable child care, they say, would bring significant numbers of mothers into the market. "If just half of the women who say they are constrained by child care went to work in the early 1990s, the labor force would gain about 850,000 workers."

The notion of providing child care so women can take jobs for little profit and honor is not particularly attractive. Nor is another argument on the Right: that welfare mothers need help getting child care because they have no business staying at home if they can be out selling hamburgers. But even though these arguments will not appeal to all of us, at least one point is getting through: that if parents are to work for their living at the miserable wages set by the market, somebody has to help them pay for their child care.

Remedies Have Little Promise

So far, the remedies offered by the Right promise little for low-income families. The tax credit for child care, expanded under Reagan, now returns to parents 20 to 30 per cent of child-care expenses, up to a total of $2,400 for one child and $4,800 for two or more. It amounts to a $3 billion annual subsidy out of a total $6.9 billion the Federal Government spends on child-care subsidies and grants.

The tax credit is only useful, obviously, to families who can afford the 70 to 80 per cent of the child-care costs not covered by the credit. The less they can afford to pay, the less the tax credit helps them.

Statistics bear out this bias: Fewer than 10 per cent of the families claiming the credit have incomes below $10,000.

For that reason, the plan proposed by George Bush—a very partial solution—is an improvement over the present situation: It would allow low-income families with at least one wage-earner to get a $1,000 tax credit for each child under four, regardless of how much they spend on child care. Families with incomes between $8,000 and $12,000 would receive the credit beginning the first year it's in effect, with the income ceiling rising over four years to $20,000.

Fading Support

For the lowest-income families, however, with insecure jobs and low, uncertain wages, direct subsidies are a high and immediate priority. One of the saddest sights has been the fading support for a bill that would have increased such subsidies. The Act for Better Child Care, supported by Michael Dukakis, would have made available $2.5 billion for states to improve the quality and quantity of child care. The ABC bill, as it's known, would have set Federal health and safety standards and provided funds to train child-care workers and increase their salaries. It would have paid for expansion of public preschool programs, to provide full-day care.

Three-fourths of the money (matched by the states) would have been set aside for subsidies: immediate relief for a significant number of parents. Under ABC, families earning up to 115 per cent of the state's median income would be technically eligible for subsidies, on a sliding scale, with priority for those on the bottom.

In California, for example, the state estimates that 20 to 25 per cent of the children who both need subsidies and are eligible for them under existing rules are actually getting them. ABC would probably double the number of subsidized children, which is now about 75,000.

The ABC bill would have been just a start at solving the child-care problem, but it would have been a start. Most important, it would have put in place a foundation for a national child-care system.

The demise of the ABC bill suggests the political shoals stranding any such broad national effort. Support was generally polarized along party lines. Republicans remain suspicious of entitlement programs and of Federal regulation.

Their suspicions have the nearly unanimous backing of business. A statement approved by the U.S. Chamber of Commerce typifies corporate concern: "Although a shortage of adequate and affordable child care may present problems in select areas of the country, the Federal Government should resist the temptation to mandate specific employee benefits, to regulate previously unregulated industries, to subsidize or compete unfairly with private-sector day-care centers, or to impose a costly and monolithic Federal child-care program."

Business—and Republicans—are both more likely to be comfortable with a Federal program like that proposed by Senator Orrin Hatch, Republican of Utah, who introduced a very modest child-care bill, authorizing $375 million for the first year (and lesser amounts for the second and third). Most of the money would have gone to states as block grants, the same unguided Reagan policy that has left child care in such disarray across the country.

Unfortunately, Republicans are not the only obstacle in the way of action for national child care. The broad base of support for the ABC bill dissolved over the issue of separation of church and state. Churches provide an estimated one-third of current child care: Would they be eligible for funds or not? To get funds, would they have to drape their statues of Mary and hire atheists as teachers?

As the bill's sponsors made compromises with the churches, the school lobby—the Parent-Teachers Association, the National Education Association— grew nervous. So did the American Civil Liberties Union. Was a precedent being set here—giving funds to churches to educate children?

And so, broad-scale child-care proposals have to wend their way through a tangled web of constitutional law, ideological contention, and economic interests. At every step of the way, child-care advocates hear (sometimes inside themselves) the more deeply emotional question: Should we be institutionalizing any system of nonparental care for our young children? We have to ask the question, but we also have to face the fact: Mothers, the traditional care-givers, are out working at paid jobs in ever greater numbers, and for many reasons, not all of them economic.

"Broad-scale child-care proposals have to wend their way through a tangled web of constitutional law."

Our society could offer many incentives to mothers or fathers to stay at home and rear children: higher wages for all those who work, including parents, so that one income would suffice; flexible hours and well-paid part-time jobs with decent benefits; parental leaves; a reform of the prevailing expectation that serious workers sacrifice their entire lives to their jobs; stricter limits on forced overtime.

So far, obtaining such concessions to parenthood has been as tough a task as legislating help for child care. We need to push for both: better child care and more time to be parents.

We will have to work for both, it seems to me, piecemeal. As the fate of even the modest ABC bill suggests, we are a long way from a national system of child care. Yale University psychologist Edward Zigler, an architect of Head Start and long-time lobbyist for child-care supports, told *Psychology Today*: "Some people are still arguing for the Swedish model—a day-care center on every corner: The government buys it and you go use it. That's unrealistic." It would cost too much: between $75 billion and $100 billion a year.

Zigler advocates building on the current school system, as some states are beginning to do in limited ways: expanding before- and after-school day care in school buildings and expanding, too, the preschool years. For children up to three, Zigler advocates a patchwork solution: infant-care leaves for parents (another measure business has been fighting in Congress) and government subsidies or a negative income tax for purchased care in the infant and toddler years. . . .

> "One reason child care has had difficulty getting on the political agenda is that those who need it most have the least time to spend lobbying for it."

One reason child care has had difficulty getting on the political agenda is that those who need it most have the least time to spend lobbying for it. And the early childhood years, when the need is most desperate and difficult to meet, are short for families with one or two children. Once they are past, it is easy to heave a sigh of relief and forget about the problem.

Greater Social Good

But we can't. We mustn't. Those of us, especially, who find satisfaction in our paid work owe a long-term debt to those who share our work as parents. If we cannot pay them what they ought to get right now, then at least we can try to see that they and others like them are paid better in the future. If we women buy our economic freedom by exploiting other women, or men, we have bought it dear indeed.

If the greater social good does not compel us to act, we have a strong private motivation. We have sons and daughters, do we not?

I watch my two-year-old, who now goes to nursery school at a cost of $5,000 a year, putting her five dollies to bed in the cradle her grandmother bought her—lining them up in a careful row, covering them head to foot with blankets and quilts.

"I have so many children," she says. "I have all these children, and so much work to do." Then she gets on her rocking horse, calls out, "Bye, bye, see you after your nap," and rides off to her job. She is already planning her future. I figure I have twenty years or so to prepare the way.

Carol Polsgrove is a member of The Progressive *magazine's editorial advisory board in Madison, Wisconsin.*

"Child-care policy must rest solidly on the recognition that the family has the primary right and responsibility to care for ... the child."

viewpoint 19

The Government's Role in Child Care Should Be Limited

Jo Ann Gasper

Child care has become an issue of public debate for the third time in this decade. It was an issue in 1980 when President Jimmy Carter held the White House Conference on Families, and again in 1984 when the U.S. House Select Committee on Children, Youth and Family held hearings. In 1988, we have the widely-publicized introduction of child-care legislation—called the Act for Better Child Care (or "ABC" bill)—by Senator Christopher Dodd (D, Conn.) and Congressman Dale Kildee (D, Michigan). The *ABC* bill has received strong support from a broad array of liberal organizations. Senator Orrin Hatch (R, Utah) has also introduced child-care legislation which is similar to the *ABC* bill.

In fact, more than 140 bills dealing with child care have been introduced in the Congress. In my judgment, most of them have problems similar to *ABC*—few recognize the importance of having *parents* control child care, rather than the government.

Children Are Pawns

Also in my judgment, the Democrats have never been reluctant to use children as political pawns in their bidding war to buy votes. That is one of the reasons why "child care" has received such public attention in the election years of 1980, 1984, and in 1988. Liberal social-engineering Democrats are expert crafters of what one observer calls the "politics of greed and envy." In national elections, they turn to "social issues" and "family policy." They do so for two reasons: liberals recognize the importance of family policy in achieving their long range goals, and they recognize the virility (if you'll pardon the word) of family issues in mobilizing constituent groups and getting voters to the polls.

Jo Ann Gasper, "The Child Care Crisis." Reprinted with permission from the *Human Life Review*, Summer 1988. © 1988 by the Human Life Foundation, Inc., 150 E. 35th Street, New York, NY 10016.

The family is obviously the basic unit of society. It is within the family that children learn the fundamental values necessary for a civilized society. The family comes before, and is therefore superior to, the State. The family determines the warp and woof of the tapestry of civilization. It is within the family that the child learns caring and sharing, and the importance of self-sacrifice. In short, it is within the family that *values* are transmitted. And, as R.H. Tawney put it (in *Religion and the Rise of Capitalism*): "The virtues of enterprise, diligence and thrift are the indispensable foundation of any complex and vigorous civilization." Only the family teaches these values. Without their transmission from one generation to the next, our culture will die.

The fragility of civilization and culture has long been recognized. From classical thinkers like Plato to modern "social planners," few would disagree that the future of a society depends on how it rears its children.

Children do indeed come with some innate abilities and natural predilections. But the family is responsible for the nurturing and *education* of children. A stable family life makes it possible for a child's natural abilities to develop, so that he (or she) can bloom into a mature, caring adult.

A child naturally seeks the truth, and values life. What parent has not been cornered by a child's third "Why?" Or not been called upon to rescue some small creature? A child's natural love for life is clearly seen in his instinctive revulsion against abortion, which I have found to be total and absolute. A child has to be "taught" by someone that killing an unborn child is not an evil. This should be easy to understand. A child instinctively identifies with the unborn child; he knows intuitively that if the unborn child is not safe in his mother's womb, then no child is safe—his *own* personal existence is endangered.

As important as child rearing is, both for the

development of the child and the future of society, it is a task best done at home by parents who can provide warm, responsive and consistent care. Dr. Raymond Moore, a developmental psychologist, and his wife Dorothy, a gifted reading specialist, point out that "There are a lot of very good nursery schools, kindergartens, and elementary schools in the world. Yet there are none whose programs can match education by loving parents of even modest ability, working with their own children in the simplest of homes."

For liberals to succeed in selling their ideas, future generations must be inculcated with radical liberal values *early*. At present, children are usually under the control of parents until they enter government schools at age 5 or 6. Although parents may leave their children in the care of others, the parents are able to set the standards, quality, and values of the care provided. Parents who must have others care for their children usually try to find someone who can provide care that is compatible with the family's values and life style. Most families, in fact, utilize informal child-care arrangements and frequently use family members. Parents, as long as they remain in control, are able to protect the values and character formation of their children. When the family's values are religiously based—and most are—parents utilize child-care arrangements which reinforce those religiously-based values. The reinforcement may be as simple as saying grace over meals or following dietary restrictions.

The importance of having strong families cannot be overestimated. It is only when there are strong families that a nation can maintain and preserve freedom. One has only to observe history to see that inevitably totalitarian states move to undermine the integrity and unity of the family. This is frequently done by separating parents and children, by encouraging children to report "unacceptable" behavior to government authorities, or encouraging children to pressure parents to do what is deemed by the government to be appropriate behavior.

The government does have a responsibility to the family. In a well-ordered society, the state will provide those things which the family itself cannot provide. It will insure freedom from foreign invasion, and provide for an economic system which will permit the family to flourish. . . .

Primary Rights of Parents

Conservatives define the family as consisting of persons who are related by blood, marriage, or adoption. Thus conservatives see the family as inherently bound with rights and responsibilities which supersede other relationships. A family is not restricted to a roof over two heads. Rather, family crosses state lines—and it extends back through history and looks forward to future generations. A family by its very nature has certain rights and

responsibilities, including the primary right and duty of parents to educate their children. The rights and responsibilities of family members are not determined by physical location but by the relationships within the family.

The political impact of the difference between the two understandings of what constitutes "family" is enormous. If "family," as liberals maintain, is not related to blood, marriage, or adoption, then the family is destroyed. The family has always been understood in the context of relationships circumscribed by birth, marriage, or legal responsibilities. The notion that family is simply a common commitment or climate that one "comes home to" would result in a radical restructuring of American society. Such an iconoclastic society would be forced to look to some other institution to be the transmitter of values and authority. This inevitably would be the government.

"The government does recognize and provide support to families."

It should be remembered that the government does recognize and provide support to families. The traditional family which has received governmental support has been based on blood, marriage, or adoption. To provide governmental support to a different kind of family would mean taxpayer support for such divergent "families" as homosexuals, cohabiting adults, or even a group of children who want to live together. . . .

The *ABC* Bill

The Democrats' major effort in 1988 to radically restructure the family is the Dodd/Kildee *ABC* bill (the "Act for Better Child Care," Senate bill 1886 and House bill 3660). Dodd and Kildee claim that:

- there is a national shortage of child care,
- the quality of child care is low and needs regulation,
- the *shortage* of child care keeps parents from jobs and training, and
- employers and the Federal government are not providing adequate resources to help parents meet their child-care needs.

These claims are both unproven and untrue—in short, myths.

Based upon such false assumptions, they have proposed legislation which would have significant consequences on the provision of child care.

The *ABC* bill will increase the cost *and* the regulation of child care while *decreasing* the supply. It would create yet another federally-funded bureaucracy, discriminate against families that choose *parental* over government care, endanger the health and development of children, and also protect low-quality child-care providers from prosecution. Worst of all, it will undermine family rights and responsibilities. Yet, the *ABC* bill is being touted as legislation "needed" to improve the quality of family life in America. . . .

Myth vs. Fact

Let us look first at the misrepresentations.

Myth: there is a national shortage of child care. True, it may be difficult for a parent to find the type of child care she *wants*, but there is no shortage of child care.

Everyone is by now familiar with the thrust of this argument for increased federal involvement. There has been a significant increase in the number of working mothers with children under six years of age. In 1950 only 12% of mothers with children under six worked. This has grown to over 50%. At the same time, the number of one-parent families, usually headed by women, has risen significantly.

These increases in "demand" are then compared with the only slight increase in the number of licensed child-care providers ("supply") to show that there is a growing shortage.

This comparison is not appropriate. Looking only at the number of "licensed" child-care providers to determine the total supply is to assume that the tip of the iceberg is all there is. But the "supply" of child care is extremely varied. Organized, licensed child-care centers are just one component. Other ways that working parents fulfill their child-rearing responsibilities include (but are not limited to) other family homes, flexible work schedules, in-home child care by a relative or other person, and working at home.

Fact: the majority of young children (over 75% of children under 5 years of age) receive care in *informal* settings. Furthermore, child care has been a rapidly-expanding industry. From 1960 to 1986 the number of children in formal group-care centers increased from 141,000 to 2.1 million—an increase of 1,500%! The number of centers increased from 4,400 to 39,929. And it is estimated that there are at least another 1.65 *million* unlicensed family day-care providers.

Regulation Is Not Better

Myth: the quality of child care is low and needs regulation. The advocates of this argument usually view unlicensed child care as low quality and think that the only "high quality" child care is provided in licensed and regulated centers. The notion that licensed centers are better than other forms of child care, or that unregulated care is by definition of poor quality, is simply wrong.

Fact: center-based care may be harmful to the health and well-being of children—and it may be particularly harmful for infants. There is no clear evidence that center care is better than informal arrangements. Rather, the evidence indicates that informal care is better for infants than formal care. Children who are cared for in centers are more likely to be exposed to infectious diseases than children cared for at home. Furthermore, the National Infant Care study funded by HHS [Department of Health and Human Services] showed that children in child-care centers received the *least* amount of adult attention, and spent the *most* time in solitary activity. And yet, in caring for small children, appropriate interaction with an adult is critical for the development of the child. Is it surprising that children cared for in their own homes have the most one-on-one activity with an adult, the least amount of time in solitary activity, and the most appropriate responses?

> *"It may be difficult for a parent to find the type of child care she* wants, *but there is no shortage of child care."*

It is certainly no surprise that most working mothers with children prefer more informal settings to center care, although it is true that better-educated mothers make greater use of organized child-care facilities for their preschool-age children than do other mothers. Over 30% of the children of employed mothers who completed four or more years of college use either day/group care or nursery/preschool as their primary child-care arrangement, compared with 15 percent for the children of employed mothers who did not complete high school.

Myth: the shortage of child care keeps low-income women from working. Advocates of a massive expansion of government control over child care and its concomitant intrusion into family responsibilities frequently argue that the lack of child care keeps low-income mothers from working and thereby causes an unnecessary burden on taxpayers. Federally-supported child care, under this erroneous assumption, would enable low-income mothers to be employed outside the home and thus reduce welfare costs.

Fact: there simply is no clear evidence that a lack of child care prevents women, especially welfare mothers, from working. There is also no clear evidence that there is a shortage of "affordable" child care. The largest federal experiment looking at the effects of welfare policies was the Seattle and Denver Income Maintenance Experiments (SIME/DIME). Researchers for SIME/DIME concluded that since low-income families utilize inexpensive or free informal arrangements, provision of free child care had no impact on their employment.

Furthermore, in an analysis of the 1970 Aid to Families with Dependent Children (AFDC) Recipient Survey, it was found that over half of the working welfare mothers of children under 14 did not take advantage of the child-care benefits available under AFDC or Title XX of the Social Security Act. Thus, a substantial number of mothers find care for their children which is either free or of minimal cost.

In addition, only four percent of unemployed women surveyed by the Census Bureau in June 1982 stated that they had turned down a job offer in the last month because of difficulties in arranging child care.

Myth: employers and the federal government are not providing adequate resources. This is probably the most dangerous of the myths. It is based on the misconception that government has a rightful role in child care. It should always be remembered that when the government becomes involved, the government ultimately will *control*, and there are endless examples of what happens when government controls.

"Government control has resulted in increasing cost and declining quality."

Look at one government-controlled service—the U.S. mail. Government mail service has resulted in increasing cost and declining quality of service. Education is another example: government control has resulted in increasing cost and declining quality. Surely our children deserve better?

Increased Employer Concern

Fact: employers have become increasingly concerned about assisting working parents. Since 1983 there has been a four-fold increase in the number of companies providing direct or indirect child-care assistance. In 1982 only some 250 companies provided child-care support to working parents. That number has grown exponentially to 3,000 in 1987. The assistance employers provide ranges from such minimal support as information and referral to on-site child-care facilities.

Employers may offer child-care vouchers as part of their compensation package, offer "flexi-time," or form consortium child-care centers. It is clear that employers are concerned about the ability of their work force to find appropriate care—the employer *and* the parent benefit from stable child care. When a working parent is pleased with the care his/her child is receiving, employee morale improves, tardiness goes down, and the employee is more stable on the job.

The federal government, through various federal programs, e.g, the dependent-care tax credit and the tax-exclusion for employers, provides taxpayer support for child care. Taxpayers are currently subsidizing child care for working parents by more than $5.7 billion a year.

Effects of Government Child Care

Given that the underlying arguments in favor of the *ABC* bill are so flawed, what are the likely results? One is that the *ABC* bill will provide taxpayer support for Yuppies (Young Upwardly-Mobile Professionals), who don't need or deserve it. For "ordinary" parents, passage of the bill will decrease the supply of child care, destroy a flexible child-care delivery system, and significantly increase costs. More mothers will be forced to leave their children for work, to keep the family financially afloat because of increased taxes. . . .

Women employed in "service" jobs show a *very low usage* (11%) of organized group-care facilities for pre-schoolers, compared with women in either managerial or professional occupations (30%). The former tend to depend more heavily on parental care, either by the women themselves or their spouses.

The *ABC* bill will most likely cause a significant reduction in the supply of child care, because it would eliminate religious programs, and would subsidize only certain types of child care rather than *all* types, both by restricting the manner of payment and by increased governmental regulation. Religiously-based providers will automatically be excluded: *ABC* clearly eliminates the eligibility of any program "that has the purpose or effect of advancing or promoting a particular religion or religion generally." Other child-care providers who do not agree with the government-mandated ideology will also be excluded. For example, Montessori schools will find it extremely difficult to meet the government class-size and age-separation restrictions. The Montessori method encourages a mixing of ages which is different from what the government will require. . . .

Furthermore, it has been shown that government purchase of services through contractual arrangements, or the delivery of services, typically has limited parental choice because of defined government specifications about service providers, methods of control, and accountability. If an acceptable government provider does not meet a parent's specific needs, there is frequently no other service arrangement available.

The fact that child-care services expand when financing methods are broadened to include vouchers, cash subsidies, and tax reductions is well documented. This permits day-care services *via* independent, family-operated, and home-based businesses.

Since the *ABC* bill will result in a child-care delivery system which is much more restrictive (i.e., funding of licensed care only), the supply of quality child care will most likely decline, and the cost of that care which is available will rise—as supply goes down, costs go up.

The entire thrust of the *ABC* bill is to move the locus of control of children from parents to government. . . .

Even such innocuous-sounding services as providing "information and referral" (I&R) will result in increased governmental control. This happens because most I&R providers will only refer to *licensed or registered* providers. The vast network of family and in-home providers will be excluded.

School-age child-care programs (typically operated by using facilities before and after school) tend to restrict private providers and thus expand the local governmental bureaucracy. And they are used to entice children out of private education into public education. This is done by permitting only the local *governmental* child-care agency to manage and operate the centers, while permitting only children who attend the school to attend the center.

These restrictions of parental choices, increased cost both for subsidized and unsubsidized child care, and increased taxes at both the state and federal levels will make it difficult for *all* parents. Mothers who would prefer to stay home will be forced to enter the work force to meet the growing costs/taxes. Already-working mothers will find child care significantly more expensive—and have greatly-reduced options.

Less Government Control

Who benefits from a government child-care program? It is clearly not parents, or children. They would be much better off with less government control and lower taxes for families with children, which would permit mothers a free choice. Parents could *choose* to work rather than be forced to work because of unfair taxation. Reduced taxes would permit parents to spend their dollars for the child care of their choice.

"Reduced taxes would permit parents to spend their dollars for the child care of their choice."

Let me say again: it is *not* "easy" for parents to find the type of care they want for their children; there are difficulties no matter what child-care arrangements are made. However, the problems are not usually "supply" problems, but rather finding care that best meets parents' needs at the right time and right price. The problem is exacerbated by the guilt that many working mothers feel when they are compelled to leave their little child in order to work.

The point is, the parental-preference problem will not be solved by federal legislation which

institutionalizes taxpayer subsidization of *restrictions* on the types of care available. Such problems can only be solved by *expanding* options and opportunities for parents.

Jeopardizing the Family

In determining what the federal or state governments can or should do to assist parents to fulfill their responsibilities, some basic principles cry out for our attention. The *foundation* of any child-care policy must rest solidly on the recognition that *the family has the primary right and responsibility to care for, nurture, educate, and protect the child.* Therefore one must be careful to insure that any governmental action will:

- strengthen the family's ability to fulfill its primary responsibilities, and *not* infringe on its natural rights;
- *not* discriminate against the family that chooses to have child care provided by a parent who stays at home;
- provide fair-and-equal treatment—including access to the various types of child-care treatment available to parents who choose non-parental care;
- use tax dollars and tax policy to support *all* families with young children, and
- establish no new government program that will increase regulations and expand the bureaucracy.

The natural family is extremely resilient: history shows that it can—and does—survive, function, and fulfill its responsibilities under very adverse circumstances. But governmental intrusion, and the undermining of family rights and responsibilities, can jeopardize the American family, and thus the very freedoms that are the American heritage.

Jo Ann Gasper served from 1981 to 1987 as deputy assistant secretary of the US Department of Health and Human Services.

"The child care tax credit would do little to increase the supply of child care or to improve its quality."

The Government Should Subsidize Child Care

Nancy Folbre and Heidi Hartmann

After decades of empty rhetoric about family values, Congress will almost certainly pass some kind of legislation to ease the burdens of working parents. Guaranteed family leave from work is also on the legislative agenda. Why now? The most obvious explanation is economic pressure. Since 1980, family income has grown only slightly despite large increases in women's participation in the labor force. Income inequality has increased. Most families have worked harder and harder simply to maintain their standard of living. Many have been seriously constrained by the persistent shortage of affordable, quality child care.

But economic factors alone don't explain the momentum behind A.B.C. [Act for Better Child Care]. Much of the credit goes to activists who kept groups like the Children's Defense Fund and the Child Care Action Coalition going in a period when their concerns were labeled politically unrealistic. No less important has been the education that feminists, trade unionists and welfare advocates received from the Reaganomics school of hard knocks.

The feminist movement, weakened by the defeat of the equal rights amendment and persistent threats to abortion rights, has developed a new appreciation of class, race and ethnic differences among women. Affirmative action, a feminist plank of the 1970s, rewarded women who could take advantage of opportunities to enter male-dominated occupations but offered little to women stuck in "pink collar" jobs as secretaries, receptionists and child care workers. Recognizing this failing, many feminist organizations began to support union organizing efforts and pay-equity campaigns.

Women of color insisted that white feminists come to grips with their own ethnocentrism, pushing

feminist politics past the rhetoric of individual rights and toward a language of social responsibility. Finally, many feminists began to recognize that they had over-idealized the world of careers. In this context, a family-policy initiative offered strategic as well as substantive benefits.

Other Advocates

The trade union movement has evolved in similar ways. Faced with declining membership and declining power, it has begun to overcome its legacy of sexism and sign up women. Union organizers have learned that women care deeply about the relationship between paid work and family work. To give just one example: Child care issues played a crucial role in the successful organizing drive among clerical workers at Harvard University.

Advocates for the poor, who bore the brunt of Federal and state budget cuts, learned that entitlement programs with a broad range of beneficiaries withstood attack. They realized that rather than splitting the poor off from everyone else, it is far better to combine redistributive policies with a new politics of fair entitlement.

The A.B.C. bill reflects all these lessons and all these constituencies. Among feminists, Representative Pat Schroeder of Colorado took the lead, organizing a Great American Family Tour in January and February 1988 to promote child care, family and medical leave, pay equity and better housing and health care. Schroeder garnered some media attention as well as an enthusiastic public response, which has helped the A.B.C. bill along. Meanwhile, the Coalition of Labor Union Women prodded the trade union movement, initiating an American Family Celebration in Washington on May 14, 1988 that rallied major unions behind an ambitious progressive family-policy agenda.

In there all along was one of the few political organizations that has consistently spoken out for

Nancy Folbre and Heidi Hartmann, "A New Politics of Entitlement," *The Nation*, October 3, 1988. Reprinted with permission of *The Nation* magazine/The Nation Company, Inc., copyright 1988.

poor people over the past decade: the Children's Defense Fund. Add in the day-to-day experience and concerns of nonprofit child care providers and you have the most important elements of the A.B.C. coalition.

Limited Assistance

Apart from some small subsidy programs such as Head Start, current Federal child care assistance is limited to an income tax credit for child care expenditures that has disproportionately benefited high-income families. The Act for Better Child Care Services would establish a Federal structure to coordinate, regulate and subsidize a decentralized child care system. It would not put Uncle Sam directly in charge of child care, as would more ambitious proposals to incorporate new programs into the public school system. But A.B.C. would depart substantially from current policy by increasing the funds available to child care providers.

Total Federal expenditures would amount to $2.5 billion a year for 1989 and the following four years. Participating state governments would match 20 percent of the total over the same period. States would set aside 15 percent of their allotment for improvements in the child care infrastructure—including improved referral systems, development and training programs for providers and increased salaries for child care workers. A maximum of 10 percent could be spent on administrative costs.

Under A.B.C., all families would be eligible for assistance on a sliding scale based on income. States would reserve 75 percent of their allotment to help subsidize families earning up to 115 percent of the state's median income (approximately the bottom 57 percent of the income distribution). In order to be eligible for subsidy, parents must hold paying jobs.

Setting Standards

A.B.C. supporters argue that the qualitative dimensions of the bill are more important than the numbers. It would set national standards for quality child care in five areas: child-staff ratios, group size, parental involvement, parental access, and health and safety. (In many states, child care is largely unregulated.) Only licensed providers at centers and home-based facilities meeting both these standards and worker training requirements would be eligible for assistance. However, many unlicensed providers would have, for the first time, a substantial incentive to apply for licenses.

The bill is far from perfect. Three concerns are particularly evident: the eligibility of some middle-income families; the bill's restriction to families in which parents hold paying jobs; and its bureaucratic component. None of these concerns are imaginary. But the bill's problems have been grossly exaggerated by conservatives who completely ignore

the pathology of "market-based" alternatives. Douglas Besharov of the American Enterprise Institute suggests that A.B.C. is a plan for middle-class self-enrichment, and Phyllis Schlafly indignantly points out that the two-earner families eligible for A.B.C. assistance have significantly higher incomes than traditional single-breadwinner families. Surprise! Two people generally earn more than one. But A.B.C. would utilize both a quota and sliding fee scale to help low- and middle-income families. It would not subsidize the affluent.

"Ideally, all parents should receive some remuneration for the socially necessary work of rearing children."

What about A.B.C.'s lack of assistance for families in which mothers don't have paying jobs? Conservatives fault the bill for encouraging mothers to work for pay. Both Schlafly and *Newsweek* economics columnist Robert Samuelson rhetorically question whether child care is superior to mother's care (father's care apparently isn't relevant). Neither expressed these fears when legislation to make paid work mandatory for many mothers receiving Aid to Families with Dependent Children was proposed.

Fixing Imbalances

Ideally, all parents should receive some remuneration for the socially necessary work of rearing children. But current tax policy discriminates particularly fiercely against families where women do double duty as care-givers and income-earners. Married homemakers, who pay neither individual income nor Social Security taxes, receive about the same social and retirement benefits as their wage-earning, tax-paying counterparts who also raise children. A.B.C. would help redress this imbalance.

What about its "bureaucratic impact"? *New York Times* columnist William Safire has warned that the A.B.C. bill would entangle child care in the tentacles of the Federal bureaucracy. Indeed, some child care providers would face higher costs to meet regulatory standards, such as minimum child-staff ratios. (Not surprisingly, much of the proprietary child care industry, including profitable firms such as Kinder-Care, is opposed to A.B.C.) But most nonprofit centers welcome some regulation as a means of enforcing high quality standards.

The market-based alternative to A.B.C., as proposed by George Bush, addresses these concerns. A tax credit of up to $1,000 per child under age 4 would be provided for families earning less than $11,000 a year (with eligibility to be raised gradually to $20,000 a year over four years). At least one family member must be employed—a nifty touch that rewards married mothers who don't work for pay but disqualifies unmarried women with children who stay home with their kids. Families could file for this tax credit whether or not they paid income taxes, and they could spend it wherever and however they wanted.

A Better Alternative

But this alternative suffers from some serious problems, as detailed in a report from Citizens for Tax Justice. Many poor families don't file income-tax returns. If they do file, they will receive a lump sum payment that amounts to only about a third of the average annual cost of child care. A family earning $10,000 in a relatively poor state, such as Maine, would fare much better under A.B.C.

"As most working parents will tell you, they need not only money but also information."

More important, the child care tax credit would do little to increase the supply of child care or to improve its quality. However liberal its rhetoric, the Bush proposal simply reiterates Reaganomic faith in the capitalist marketplace. Its basic presupposition is that the child care market works just fine—low-income parents just need a little more money to spend in it. But as most working parents will tell you, they need not only money but also information, high quality standards and a structure that enables them to shape the child care program in their communities. These needs could be addressed, if not completely satisfied, by something as simple as A.B.C.

Nancy Folbre is staff economist at the Center for Popular Economics, an organization which provides economics education for activists, labor unions, and other interested groups. Heidi Hartmann is director of the Institute for Women's Policy Research, a think tank on public policy issues in Washington, DC.

"Millions of fulltime mothers are forced to subsidize employed mothers."

The Government Should Offer Tax Credits for Child Care

Phyllis Schlafly

Why are families with children short of cash? Because their tax burden has dramatically increased!

In 1948, an average couple with two children paid 2% of annual income in federal taxes. In 1988, an average couple with two children paid 24% of annual income in federal taxes. Families need tax relief—not government handouts! They want to spend their own money—not be told how to spend subsidies.

Child care bills. . . . can be grouped into two types of legislative options: (1) The liberal Dodd-Kennedy (ABC) daycare bills to subsidize licensed centers, impose regulations, and discriminate against family care. (2) The Child Tax Credit plan to assure parental choice in child care. This plan was pioneered by Congressmen Clyde Holloway, Richard Schulze, and Philip Crane, and Senators Malcolm Wallop and Pete Domenici, and is advocated by President George Bush.

The liberal child care action plan would—

1. Increase taxes.

2. Create a federal baby-sitting bureaucracy.

3. Discriminate against mothers who take care of their own children.

4. Discriminate against relatives who take care of children out of love and without pay.

5. Impose federal regulations and control that will
   • interfere with the curriculum of religious daycare,
   • cause legal harassment of religious daycare,
   • raise dramatically the cost of neighborhood daycare,
   • drive low-cost daycare out of business or underground,
   • reduce availability and affordability of daycare.

6. Discriminate against low-income families by subsidizing
   • upper-income families,
   • with two-earner couples,
   • who put their children in secular daycare centers.

7. Lead to a federal daycare system with a potential tax cost of $100 billion annually.

8. Reward agencies that are paid for daycare services but penalize families that take care of their children out of love and commitment without payment.

9. Lead to a society modeled on Sweden where most children are cared for in government institutions.

The Alternative

The pro-family solution to the cost of child care is to give a tax credit for each child. This pro-family plan would—

1. Assure 100% parental freedom of choice in child care. Therefore, it would not substitute government decisions or incentives for parental choices.

2. Not discriminate against mothers who take care of their own children.

3. Not discriminate against or require the licensing or registration of grandmothers or other relatives.

4. Put 100% of the available cash in the hands of parents instead of bureaucrats, regulators, and providers.

5. Not build a federal baby-sitting bureaucracy.

6. Relieve some of the present unfair tax burden on families with children.

7. Help low-income families proportionately more than higher-income.

8. Move toward tax reduction instead of tax increases and costly bureaucratic growth.

Phyllis Schlafly, "The Challenge of Child Care Costs," *The Phyllis Schlafly Report,* February 1989. Reprinted with permission.

9. Not interfere with religious daycare or cause lawsuits or harassment.
10. Not raise the costs of neighborhood daycare.
11. Preserve local control over daycare licensing standards.

What Is the Child Tax Credit?

A $1,000 income tax credit per child under age 5,* up to a limit of 3 children, in families with at least one parent employed,** with an annual income under $21,000.*** (Options: $25,000 or $36,000.) This would reduce a family's income tax up to $3,000 per year.

*Note that this credit is for every child, regardless of whether he is at home, grandmother's, Aunt Millie's, neighborhood daycare mother's, church facility, or center.

**The requirement that at least one parent be employed means: (1) Families where *only* one parent is employed will *not be* discriminated against. (The liberal bills would deny all benefits unless the mother is employed and uses paid institutional licensed daycare.) (2) The child care issue is *not* about welfare! Mothers on welfare are already entitled under existing law to full compensation for daycare expenses at the market rate in their locality. In addition, the federal government spends $3 billion for various programs for child care for low-income mothers.

***Note that this plan is directed at low-income families. The income cap would move upwards as funds become available.

The Options

The Child Tax Credit plan has 3 options:

Option A

Target: Families with children under age 5
Tax credit: $1,000 per child—limit of 3 children
Income cap: $21,000
Phase-in: in the first year, only families earning less than $15,000 would receive some benefit. Dependent care credit unaffected except for families that get the child tax credit.

Option B

Target: Families with children under age 5
Tax credit: $1,000 per child—limit of 3 children
Income cap: $26,000
Phase-in: in the first year, only families earning less than $15,000 would receive some benefit. Dependent care credit eliminated for families with income above $50,000.

Option C

Target: Families with children under age 5
Tax credit: $1,000 per child—limit of 3 children
Income cap: families earning less than $36,000 would receive some benefit
Phase-in: in the first year, families earning less than

$18,000 would receive full benefit. Option C gradually eliminates the current dependent care tax credit and replaces it with a universal tax credit for low- and moderate-income families with young children.

How will the child care tax credit help low-income families who pay little or no taxes?

Low-income families will benefit through an expansion of the earned income tax credit (EITC). The EITC is already a proven formula and successful part of our tax system. It rewards work by low-income people by returning to them some or all of the money they pay in taxes. Working parents who have no income tax liability will have a share of their Social Security taxes returned to them without losing Social Security benefits.

Low-income families who currently receive the earned income tax credit (EITC) at 14% of earnings would benefit through an extension of the EITC. Families earning below $7,000 would receive benefits amounting to 28% of earnings if they have one child under age 5, or 40% of earnings if they have two or more children under age 5. As income rises above $7,000, benefits would be incrementally reduced until the credit reaches $1,000 per child.

Ending Discrimination

Will families have to wait until the end of the year to receive the funds from their tax credit?

No. They can simply fill out a government form to adjust their withholding statement so that less money is taken out of their paycheck each week. The EITC would provide cash assistance to very low-income working parents which they would receive through their weekly paychecks.

"ANY type of subsidy or grant program means starting a new federal bureaucracy that will grow into a bureaucratic nightmare which will be unjust."

How will the tax credit plan be funded?
By partially phasing out the current dependent care tax credit, which is highly discriminatory against families with a mother in the home and benefits primarily upper-income two-earner couples.

Can we support legislation that includes both a Child Tax Credit and subsidies for daycare centers?
Absolutely not! We cannot accept ANY subsidies, grants, vouchers, certificates, loans, or credits that discriminate against care of children in their own homes by their own mother or other relatives. This type of discrimination is NOT acceptable! Furthermore, ANY type of subsidy or grant program means starting a new federal bureaucracy that will grow

into a bureaucratic nightmare which will be unjust, discriminatory, intrusive in family well-being, and terribly costly.

Does the Child Tax Credit meet pro-family criteria? The Child Tax Credit approach is the only plan that meets the criteria of Executive Order 12606 on "The Family" issued September 2, 1987.

• Does this action by government strengthen or erode the stability of the family, and particularly, the marital commitment?

• Does this action strengthen or erode the authority and rights of parents in the education, nurture, and supervision of their children?

• Does this action help the family perform its functions, or does it substitute government activity for the function?

• Does this action by government increase or decrease family earnings? Do the proposed benefits of this action justify the impact on the family budget?

• Can this activity be carried out by a lower level of government or by the family itself?

The Liberal Plan

Child Care Review, the leading journal for the daycare industry, has reported that the Dodd ABC federal daycare bill would actually cost parents nearly $1.2 billion in additional payments and displace over 786,000 children now in licensed facilities. According to this study, the Dodd ABC bill would have the effect of closing 12,600 daycare centers, or 20.3 percent of all the licensed facilities now in operation, because of the cost increases resulting from the bill.

"The federal standards mandated in the ABC bill would raise the cost of licensed care."

The magazine explained that the federal standards mandated in the ABC bill would raise the cost of licensed care and displace children because daycare is such a labor-intensive industry. With staff costs already accounting for 51 percent (or $27.18) of the parents' weekly daycare cost, federal standards that would impose lower staff-to-child ratios than are now required by state regulations would dramatically raise parents' costs in most states. (The ABC bill is an attempt to impose on all 50 states the staff-to-child ratios now in effect in such states as Connecticut and Massachusetts, the home states of the bill's sponsors.)

Significantly, the two states which lead the nation in available licensed child care, Texas and Florida, would be the hardest hit by federal staffing standards, according to the report. Texas parents

could expect an average increase in daycare costs of $13.59 per week, and Florida parents could expect an average increase of $16.21 per week. The cost increases for infant care would be much higher. . . .

The Current Status

The current Dependent Care Tax Credit should be phased out because it is unjust and discriminatory. The dependent care credit is an income tax credit of up to 30% of money actually spent for daycare for children under age 13, for a maxmum of two children. The maximum credit that can be claimed is $720 for one child, $1,440 for two or more children.

This Dependent Care Tax Credit is denied to families that have a fulltime mother.

This Dependent Care Tax Credit is worthless to low-income families with little or no tax liability. This Dependent Care Tax Credit is worthless to families who use child care by relatives to whom little or no cash payment is made.

The Dependent Care Tax Credit is highly discriminatory because millions of fulltime mothers are forced to subsidize employed mothers, and millions of low-income families are forced to subsidize the two-income middle- and upper-income families who use 80% of the dependent care tax credit.

The earned income tax credit (EITC) should be expanded because it is a proven and popular formula in our current tax system. The EITC rewards people for working instead of for not working. Low-income employed families with children receive cash benefits through the EITC, which encourage them to work harder and discourage dependence on other welfare programs. The EITC is the opposite of current welfare spending which rewards people for *not* working. The earned income tax credit is a conservative and pro-family concept.

Phyllis Schlafly has been a leading conservative writer in the controversies over working women and child raising. She publishes The Phyllis Schlafly Report *monthly.*

"Anyone who has tried to balance one life as the mother of a family with another...in the workplace knows... the absolute primacy of the first."

Feminism Undermines the Family

Ruth R. Wisse

When the women's movement began to show some muscle in the late 60's and early 70's, I decided it was a passing fad, like the hula hoop. It did not seem possible to me that ideas in such obvious contradiction of the facts should be able to inspire and propel a serious mass movement. Convinced that women were the practical gender, I was sure they would never be deceived by false ideology, and I expected the movement to evaporate as quickly as it had materialized. It was the worst cultural prediction of my life.

The women's movement first appeared to me in the form of Farla Kronenberg (not her real name). Farla's younger sister had been my bunkmate at camp from the time we were eight, and I guess that Farla and I were originally drawn together in dumb protest against the unfairness of life's endowments. Her sister had been the most beautiful girl at camp and later the carnival queen of our high school: confident that her natural appeal would never be diminished no matter how many smiles she lavished, she won the heart of every boy within a four-year radius. It was bad enough for me, who only had this glorious girl as a temporary summer roommate. My sympathy for Farla, who had her forever, knew no bounds.

I actually preferred Farla to her younger sister. She was not bad-looking by normal standards, and she had a critical vigor that made her seem even smarter than she was. For a time when we were undergraduates at McGill she took me on as her junior debating partner, and in more than one collegiate meet her wit proved our sharpest weapon. While her sister joined a sorority, became engaged to a stellar young man of good family, and continued to radiate like the sun, Farla became something of a

campus celebrity, with her own weekly column in the school paper and an interview show on a local radio station.

She seemed, however, very stupid about boys. She sniped at those who liked her, and mooned over the handsome fraternity types who ignored her, not the way some of us would develop a secret crush on a boy and whisper our dream into the pillow, but willfully and publicly. She would invite one of these haughty upperclassmen to host a party she intended to give and when he turned her down she would promptly ask him to a movie or a concert, so that he had to say no and no and sometimes no again before she gave up. Later, when the engagements and marriages started in our circle, she would turn up at parties in provocative dresses and talk so grossly about the physical properties of her date of the moment that you knew she had no hope of enjoying them. Then, a year out of college, she married a fellow she had met the previous month at a wedding in New Jersey. His name was Martin, but she always called him Angel, a comment on his beauty but also, I fear, on the scanty physical impression he was making on her. Within the year he was firmly lodged in her father's business and in her friends' beds. Long before men had turned into the kind of primping fashion plates some of them have since become, I was present when Martin and Farla showed up at a party and the hostess greeted them with, "Oh, Marty, what a beautiful suit!"

Enter the Mystique

It was Farla, then, in the first years of her marriage, who invited me to read Betty Friedan's *The Feminine Mystique.* The book, she said, defined everything that was going wrong in her own life, and clarified the problem of contemporary women. Since at the time I too was riddled with plenty of doubts about the quality and meaning of my life, I took up the book eagerly, looking for the

Ruth R. Wisse, "Living with Women's Lib." Reprinted from *Commentary,* August 1988 by permission; all rights reserved.

enlightenment that she claimed to have found in it.

I read: "The feminine mystique says that the highest value and the only commitment for women is the fulfillment of their own femininity." American society, including in the form of women's magazines and Madison Avenue, had cultivated and fostered this mystique, making the housewife feel guilty if she aspired to anything beyond her daily drudgery. Psychotherapy assisted in the fraud. Freud, in whose Vienna women had been denied all opportunities to realize their full potential, developed theories rationalizing this culturally-induced condition and making it seem inevitable. Although feminists and suffragettes had won the fight for civic equality, they had been defeated by the mystique which prevented women from practicing it. And so forth, chapter after chapter.

"The dissatisfaction . . . ascribed to women's confinement in the female role was actually the result of their liberation from that role."

I was stunned. This was demagoguery not about subjects I was used to—Jews, the middle class—but about women, and it caught me by surprise. The very term "mystique," with its sinister overtones, implied that women were being manipulated by powers outside themselves, insidious forces of persuasion, distortion, and oppression. But to what did the term actually correspond? Why should the actions of women, the *choices* of women, be attributed to something beyond themselves? I knew that I and every other woman around me— particularly those of the older generation—were persons of independent will and firm character. In fact, both in my own extended family and among the families of my friends, I had rarely known anything but female-dominated households; quite a number of these families, including mine, bore the names of female ancestors. Yet here was Betty Friedan describing an entire sex of victims. It seemed to me that in the name of sisterly compassion she was actually expressing contempt, putting women down as victims of fate, rather than partners in the human drama, so that she could pretend to come to their rescue.

Inverting the Problem

Of course she was on to something important. By the beginning of the 60's, World War II almost forgotten, and American prosperity in full swing, a healthy, fairly well-to-do woman like Betty Friedan could raise her children in unprecedented peace and plenty without exhausting her energy or ruining her body. Suddenly the role of mother and nurturer had

been lightened almost to the point of weightlessness, incidentally by the very family-oriented market forces Betty Friedan deplored. The fact of raising a family, which throughout human history had figured as a woman's most important contribution to society, was now no longer enough to occupy more than half her life—with diaper services, maybe, even less than that. On top of this, overpopulation was becoming a great issue, and women began to be made as aware of their sudden superfluity as of their abundant spare time and beckoning opportunities.

Yet even then I could see plainly that Betty Friedan had inverted the terms of the problem. The dissatisfaction that she ascribed to women's confinement in the female role was actually the result of their liberation from that role. The restlessness that she documented in women like herself derived from one of the most radical changes in human history—the expectation that one could raise in health and safety as many children as one could bear. In my endless discussions with Farla I pointed out that I myself was the child of a twelfth or thirteenth child on my mother's side, a ninth child on my father's side, while each of her parents had about a dozen living and dead siblings as well. Both my mother and hers had lost a child before we were born; their greatest dream must have been to keep *us* alive, knowing as they did how fragile children were, how much luck and skill it took to nurture them to full maturity. If women now, after the great Depression, after the world war, and, in the case of our two families, after harrowing escapes from Europe, had been granted the gift of long life both for themselves and their children, the only thing they could be suffering was the syndrome Erich Fromm had dubbed the "escape from freedom."

Too Much Freedom

Not long before reading *The Feminine Mystique*, I had read Primo Levi's account of Auschwitz, and a passage in his book *If This Is a Man* (later renamed *Survival in Auschwitz*) kept recurring to me. I copied it out to show to Farla:

> For human nature is such that grief and pain—even simultaneously suffered—do not add up as a whole in our consciousness, but hide, the lesser behind the greater, according to a definite law of perspective. It is providential and is our means of surviving in the camp. And this is the reason why so often in free life one hears it said that man is never content. In fact it is not a question of a human incapacity for a state of absolute happiness, but of an ever-insufficient knowledge of the complex nature of the state of unhappiness; so that the single name of the major cause is given to all its causes, which are composite and set out in an order of urgency. And if the most immediate cause of stress comes to an end, you are grievously amazed to see that another one lies behind; and in reality a whole series of others.
>
> So that as soon as the cold, which throughout the winter had seemed our only enemy, had ceased, we

became aware of our hunger; and repeating the same error we now say: "If it was not for the hunger! . . ."

Levi has this habit of distilling general human truths from his unprecedented personal experience, and this particular definition of unhappiness seemed to me highly appropriate to our situation, mine and Farla's. Was not the "women's problem" a symptom of the relative ease of our lives, our dissatisfaction—the intelligent animal's vital sign—a tribute to the fact that we were no longer burdened with our parents' struggle for survival? I did not say this made our problems less acute, but they were the problems of greater choice, richer liberty. In offering up the passage from Primo Levi's book, I suspect I was also trying to remind Farla of our miraculous privilege, for her family had come to Canada from Germany not long before we ourselves arrived in 1940, and they too constituted a tiny remnant of a once-vast clan.

Against Our Will

I was genuinely puzzled by Farla's resistance to my argument, written on her face as I spoke. There we sat with our babies in the park, which is just where I wanted to be. Farla and I had part-time jobs, and *au pair* girls living at home to take care of the children when we were out. We were constantly complaining to each other about the unending series of interruptions to our well-made schedules; and though I am ashamed to confess it, we were still spinning sexual fantasies more appropriate to teen-agers than to mothers. But I still assumed that for Farla, as for me, these irritations were inevitable imperfections in an otherwise blessed existence. And if not blessed, then ours to change. If you don't want this kind of life, I said, why don't you do something else? Take on a full-time housekeeper and a full-time job, if not immediately then when Jonathan goes to nursery school. Can you really suppose it was the feminine mystique that made you want to marry, made you choose your husband, made you have your baby? Had you read Betty Friedan's book earlier, would you have acted otherwise?

Farla dismissed me impatiently. It was not simply a question of her personal happiness, she said, but of sexual discrimination. (Our talk began to resemble one of our college debates, except that now we were on opposing sides.) Could I not see the larger issue at stake—the liberation of women from the demeaning images that relegated them to a permanently inferior status? Why should women make the beds and sit in the park while men made the money and sat on the bench? Who determined the roles of "motherhood" and "fatherhood" in the first place? The relative happiness I had spoken of was dictated by relative expectations, and my satisfactory adjustment to motherhood was only a response to conditioning. Levi's words were applicable, indeed—for he was explaining the condition of slaves forced to scramble for crumbs at the hands of their masters. My contentment, too, was that of a slave, but one who did not recognize her enslavement and therefore thought she was free. Consciousness of abuse was the necessary first step toward its correction. If I resisted the idea of the new feminism it was because I was so thoroughly part of the problem I did not even know what it was to seize control of one's own destiny.

These last phrases struck a nerve. Farla had invited me to read Betty Friedan's book because it spoke to the problems of our lives. When I told her that it did not speak to the problem of *my* life, her confidence was shaken not in the book but in me. The tautology implicit in the term "mystique" became explicit as I saw myself being reduced to a pawn in Farla's theory. In order, presumably, to set me free, she was denying me the freedom of a rational, thinking being. I can't believe that you want to turn sex into ideology, I said incredulously. This totalitarian language—you are either part of the problem or part of the solution—is just a crude adaptation of the Marxist analysis of class conflict, which is crude enough already. Besides, if women are now the oppressed proletariat, do you intend to launch a revolution to free us from our chains? And if we would rather cultivate our bourgeois lives, are we going to have to be reeducated against our will? . . .

"In order, presumably, to set me free, she was denying me the freedom of a rational, thinking being."

What could one offer against those who are prepared to define womanhood as a "problem" capable of "solution," or to represent the female as a sex that has to be compensated for past injustices? How, for that matter, can one ask young people to assume, and enjoy, the differentiated responsibilities of men and women when each sex longs to prolong its androgynous childhood forever?

Our parents faced no such problem. When I was sixteen, I wanted to be a war correspondent or a trucker. I wanted to play boys' basketball, not girls'. I announced that I would never marry, never compromise my independence. My mother, who had been a rebel in a much more radical age than mine, responded simply, *"Bay yidn zaynen nishto kayn nones"*—"we Jews have no nuns." Thus she instructed me that celibacy even in its most exalted sublimations was not one of my options. I was expected to find a husband, to procreate, and to nurture a family. Nothing personal, just the law and the custom.

Humiliating as it was to be reduced to a formula—and trust my mother to find one that stung!—I think I was grateful even then for the utter certainty of her expectations. She *knew* what was good for me, and did not have to waste her breath on arguments. My protest, too, was the expected thing, the inevitable resistance to maturity—and to be dismissed as such. Three years later I was engaged to be married, and although my haste had other causes than these, I do not doubt that I have my mother as well as my husband to thank for my good fortune.

Without a Firm Voice

That firm voice of my mother's is hard to fake. The modern parent, duly attentive to social order *and* individual self-expression, aware of biological determinism *and* social conditioning, persuaded by the right to happiness in the here and now as well as by civilization's just demand that gratification be postponed, is not so well placed to be a firm guide. Midge Decter, who was the first to see that the problems of women today stem from freedom rather than oppression, has also written the book on what kind of guidance we liberal parents do manage to give our children, and with what sorry results. "You really don't have to get married if you don't want to," says the liberal parent to her daughter, "though you might regret it later if you don't. You should prepare for any career you like, including ones that have been traditionally closed to women, but on the other hand you might want to look for something that can be combined with family life, just in case you do decide to get married and have children. A war correspondent sounds like a terrifically important job, especially if you are one of the few who still believe that there are things worth fighting for, but what will you do with your babies in the bunker? As for trucking, it might make nursing difficult. Have you considered architecture or horticulture?"

"Happy is the woman whose husband is prepared to carry the economic burden of the family during at least her child-rearing years."

And yet I wish I could assume my mother's authority because I know she was right. The infinite freedom and extended life span that middle-class women now enjoy has not fundamentally altered their biological or social priorities, because the period when women are maximally attractive and healthy and vigorous is still the same as it was, and not likely to change. The mysterious part of life—marriage and procreation—still requires the kind of

foolhardy courage that is associated with youth; those who postpone and postpone until they are "ready" find that life is shorter than the time they need to prepare for it.

As for the social implications of the argument, since the biological differences between women and men suggest differentiated functions, any society that intends to maintain its balance does well to take its cue from the guidelines of nature. Happy is the woman whose husband is prepared to carry the economic burden of the family during at least her child-rearing years, and those who have enjoyed such protective blessings are nothing short of wicked when, explicitly or implicitly, they contrive to destroy the fragile contract that promotes them. . . .

There is no way of avoiding the anxiety that results from the vast opportunities middle-class women now enjoy. Anyone who has tried to balance one life as the mother of a family with another—either in tandem or in sequence—as an equal competitor in the workplace knows the wrenching difficulties involved. What made it easier for me, and for most women of my generation, was our certainty about the relative significance of these "roles," both in our own lives and in the social fabric, the absolute primacy of the first, the incidental importance of the second. We inherited this certainty, but most of us would go on to reconfirm it on the basis of our own experience.

Thanks to Farla and her like, and all who have come after her, this is no longer the case. Yet when I think of the children I have raised, and the home I have cradled, and the enmeshment of pleasure that has issued forth from these most primitive and exalted responsibilities, it seems to me utterly depraved to go weighing the privilege of motherhood on the scale of "power," or to go totting up the balance of so much motherhood versus so much professional or working life. I can only pray that my daughter and my prospective daughters-in-law, as well as all the female students I cherish and respect, will understand this, too, though the odds are against them in the ideologically poisoned atmosphere in which they have grown up, and what with the hesitation of mothers like me to clean it up.

Ruth R. Wisse is a professor of Yiddish literature at McGill University in Montreal, Canada.

Feminism Does Not Undermine the Family

Susan Cohen and Mary Fainsod Katzenstein

The War over the Family, In Defense of the Family, and *Rethinking the Family* are but a few of the books produced over the last decade in the political encounters between feminists and traditionalists. Curiously, the battle is not fundamentally about the family, but rather a conflict over the roles and relationships of men and women. Moreover, the differences of opinion over the needs and interests of children constitute a skirmish more than a war. This essay advances an argument: Feminists and traditionalists disagree deeply about issues fundamental to the nature of society and the role of men and women within it. Finding a middle ground is neither easy nor perhaps even possible. But to say that the controversy is over who is pro- or antifamily obscures rather than illuminates the issue. The debate is fundamentally about the places in society of men and women. . . .

Feminism and the traditionalist Right are terms that require definition if our discussion is to proceed. When we speak of feminism and the Right, we will be distinguishing between two theoretical perspectives that are themselves extraordinarily heterogeneous. By feminist views, we refer to arguments that start from the premise that society now and in the past has been arranged hierarchically by gender and that such arrangements must be challenged. . . .

By rightist, traditional, or conservative views (we use the terms interchangeably), we refer to writings of wide-ranging perspectives on the economic, social, and moral responsibility of the state to its citizens. What these writings share is a belief either in the different natures of men and women, or in the desirability of a continued division of labor by gender whatever might be the similarity or difference in men and women's nature. Thus the writings of the New Right speak of the religious and biologically mandated differences in the life callings of men and women. Neoconservatives, by contrast, emphasize the desirability of gender-neutral, nonintrusive laws that afford equal educational and job opportunities for men and women even as they "prefer" that women elect different life priorities from those men choose. Absolutely central to both views is the assumption that the government has now done all it can do, that virtually all antidiscrimination laws that might provide guarantees of equal opportunity are now in place.

The Traditional Family

Diverse as different components of the Right are, they are united around an idealization of the traditional nuclear family. Contained in this idealization is a particular view of men's and women's roles that is absolutely crucial to an understanding of the ideological divide between feminism and the Right.

The Right's view of gender roles is remarkably invariant across neoconservative and New Right positions. A man's responsibility to his family is best met by his success in the market, his ability as a wage earner to support his wife and children; a woman's worth is measured by her dedication to her role as wife and mother. This case is made with evangelical conviction by Phyllis Schlafly in *The Power of the Positive Woman* and *The Power of the Christian Woman*. Motherhood is a woman's calling. If a woman wants love, emotional, social, or financial security, or the satisfaction of achievement, no career in the world can compete with motherhood. That is not to say that women can never find fulfillment outside the home. The rare woman (Mother Theresa is one example that Schlafly offers) may find fulfillment in life's other options, and some may successfully pursue both marriage

Susan Cohen and Mary Fainsod Katzenstein, "The War Over the Family Is Not Over the Family," in *Feminism, Children, and the New Families*, edited by Sanford M. Dornbusch and Myra H. Strober. New York: The Guilford Press, 1988. Reprinted with permission.

and career. But this pursuit of dual responsibilities is possible only if two conditions are met: (1) if a woman relies on her own resourcefulness rather than expecting others, the government in particular, to come to her assistance; and (2) if she does not allow her primary role as wife and mother to be superseded by other interests or responsibilities. Here Schlafly offers the example of "Mrs." Thatcher, who managed both to become Prime Minister of Great Britain and to cook breakfast every morning for her husband (in contrast to Mrs. Betty Ford "who stayed in bed while her husband cooked his own breakfast during the many years he was Congressman").

Brigitte Berger and Peter Berger, who have written in defense of the bourgeois family from a neoconservative perspective, are less proselytizing but no less convinced:

> Individual women will have to decide on their priorities. Our own hope is that many will come to understand that life is more than a career and that this "more" is above all to be found in the family. But however individual women decide, they should not expect public policy to underwrite and subsidize their life plans.

The emphasis on the primacy of motherhood and the secondary concession to women's other sources of identity and fulfillment (as long as women don't expect any special help) are common to New Right and neoconservative perspectives alike. . . .

Which Family?

While the Right idealizes the traditional nuclear family in which the man works for wages and the woman stays home to raise the children, feminists reject the claim that this particular version of family life is the only acceptable form. As Barrie Thorne says in her introduction to *Rethinking the Family*, "Feminists have challenged beliefs that any specific family arrangement is natural, biological, or 'functional' in a timeless way." Thus if one is asking who is for the family and who against it, one must also ask, "Which family?"

A profound disagreement between the Right and feminists does exist—one that focuses on the relationship of women to the family. It is this, rather than the debate over the needs and interests of children, that has fueled the feminist-Right conflagrations. . . .

In the struggle between feminists and the Right the family has been a battleground, but it is not, in fact, the real source of conflict. Feminism is not antifamily; the Right is not simply pro-family. To recognize that there has been a misnaming of the issue is, we hope, to introduce a note of calm into the conflict, a conflict that has frequently been tinged with hysteria. There *are* serious, deep differences between feminism and the Right. These cannot be minimized. However, there are differences not primarily over what children need or whether the family ought to be abolished, but over the place of men and women in society. Looking past the turmoil, one finds this common ground: an acceptance of the family as an arrangement that is, at least potentially, productive for the human spirit as well as the body, and a recognition that all children need stable affectionate care.

Female Autonomy

Where feminists and conservatives part ways, often bitterly, is over the traditional sexual division of labor. In a fundamental sense this question of gender roles is a question about autonomy.

"Autonomy" is a term often heard in liberal democracies, and in this country both feminism and the Right claim to value it highly. But it is a protean word. One finds widely varying notions about what it means, who has a right to it, in what ways, and what it has to do with public policy. Conservatives, many of whom are in reality laissez-faire liberals, tend to think in terms of "being left alone." Feminists, on the other hand, are far more likely to hold government responsible for giving people *tools* for autonomy; public policy is to increase life-options.

The central question today, of course, is autonomy for women. Recognizing that neither feminism nor the Right represents monolithic entities, we generalize in the following way: The New Right sees a natural sexual order outside the realm of autonomy; in it, biology determines how we live. What it mandates for women is not only the physical act of giving birth but a female essence, a female place in society, flowing almost entirely from that physical act (or the capacity for it) and from the rearing that follows childbirth. The neoconservative Right avoids the implication that biology is destiny. Women and men are said to choose their destiny, to affect through individual effort and talent the course of their own life careers. Yet both implicitly and explicitly, neoconservatives express their expectations that men and women will choose differently.

"If one is asking who is for the family and who against it, one must also ask, 'Which family?'"

Feminists, with the exception of those such as Shulamith Firestone, gracefully, often joyfully, accept the gift of biology, but respond to it so as to preserve women's autonomy as much as possible. The capacity to bear children is seen as a gift to be used when motherhood is genuinely desired; it should not mean an unwanted child. Most feminists are reluctant to draw neobiological conclusions from biological facts. That is to say, having the capacity for childbirth says little about who one is or how one is to find meaning in life or what sort of freedom one has or should have. Although feminists such as Jean Elshtain are exceptions, most feminists assiduously avoid the advocacy of a social or moral division of labor lest it appear to evoke the traditional strictures of biological destiny.

Reshaping the Family

With the exception of radical thinkers like Kate Millet and Firestone, most feminists believe that a large measure of autonomy is possible for women, whether they are mothers or not, within the confines of the nuclear (not necessarily heterosexual or dual-parenting) family. The traditional family has to be rethought and refashioned. Feminist visions of the family are far more varied than the vision of the family that is idealized by the Right (in which the woman meets her destiny by channeling all energy into motherhood). Feminism calls on people to give up such cherished but mistaken notions as: all women have a vocation in motherhood; a child needs constant care from her or his biological mother; lesbians are morally inferior mothers; men aren't suited to be the nurturers of small children. A sharing of child care and household tasks, and day care arrangements in which there is stable, affectionate attention, are two ways in which family life can be reshaped so as to make it possible to be both a woman and a person who is economically, politically, psychologically, and spiritually autonomous.

Susan Cohen is a Ph.D. candidate and Mary Fainsod Katzenstein is an associate professor in the government department at Cornell University in Ithaca, New York.

"Women admired and served men not because that's their nature, but because tradition and male power shaped women's choices and behaviors."

Women Are Victims of Sexism

Lucia A. Gilbert

It still surprises me when I see blue and pink bows Scotch-taped to the heads of newborn babies displayed in hospital nurseries. This example, trivial as it may be, reflects a larger and very important reality. Biological sex makes a difference in our society and in many ways gets emphasized from the moment of birth. Parents raise girls to be kind, loving, and nurturing. Parents and teachers alike expect girls to be well-behaved, neat, and orderly, and they comment when girls act otherwise. Their future is pretty well mapped out—girls eventually marry and have children. My daughter was first proposed to when she was five. The checkout man at the grocery store asked her to marry him and promised he would wait for her to grow up. She has probably received an average of five proposals a year since that time.

The cartoon strip "Cathy" reminds us daily that many women believe they need men desperately. Cathy's thoughts center on filling her "inner space"—either with food or through a relationship with a man that brings eventual motherhood. She feels incomplete without a man and poignantly plays out in an exaggerated way common views of women's dependency on men.

Boys, on the other hand, are socialized to develop freedom of spirit, independence, and self-directedness. In contrast to their expectations for girls, parents and teachers expect boys to break the rules, be indifferent about their attire, and let others pick up after them. Their future is also mapped out—to be successful in careers and have a family. How cute boys are is far less important than how talented or smart they are. Boys rarely receive proposals of marriage from checkout women at the grocery store.

But are the sexes truly "opposite"? In reality, there are few, if any, ways in which women and men are really opposite. Different, yes; opposite, no. For instance, as babies, males and females cry about the same, but as adults, women generally cry more than men. The sexes learn to express emotions in somewhat different ways, but both sexes possess the capacity to cry. Weight provides another good example. Women typically diet more than men, although a comparable proportion of women and men fall into the "overweight" category. This difference in their dieting behavior does not come about because women occupy the fat end of the weight continuum and men the thin end. Rather, for reasons connected with socialization and body image, women worry more about the extra pounds. Generally speaking, men feel less pressure to achieve a svelte look.

No Real Opposition

Nonetheless, we unwittingly use the term "opposite sex" and act *as if* women and men fundamentally differ. We learn from an early age that the attributes that describe girls should not describe boys, and vice versa. Incorrect assumptions based on stereotypes lead us to believe that women are dependent and emotional, men are not and should not be; men are independent and unfeeling, women are not and should not be. The stereotypic list goes on and on. Women are intuitive, weak, and virtuous; men are rational, strong, and capable of deceit. Women take care of children and the home; men take care of women and children and the world outside the home.

The expression "opposite sex" implies even more—that women and men presumably act in opposition to one another. It suggests an underlying antagonism or basic conflict—the pitting of one sex against the other—men against women, women against men, the proverbial battle of the sexes. All too often we hear comments intimating that women "catch men," "hook men," and devote their lives to

Lucia Gilbert, *Sharing It All*. New York: Plenum Publishing Corporation, 1988. Reprinted with permission.

trying to change men's erring and irresponsible ways. Men, according to the lore, fear "losing their independence," "getting tied down," and being "hooked" by women. . . . Because women supposedly need men more than men need women, they must continually strive to understand men in order to hold on to them. . . .

Female Dependency

> I wanted to write about a girl in love—not just with a man, but with the world.

This statement about a 17-year-old heroine in the novel *Rich in Love* alludes to the limitations society sometimes places on women. The author wanted to present an adolescent who goes beyond the stereotype, one capable of mastering the intrinsically healthy conflict between her desire for security and dependence and her thirst for novelty, adventure, and independence.

To a large degree women have been conditioned to focus their lives around men. Their efforts to act autonomously and to broaden their interests and activities beyond the sphere of the family were met with great skepticism historically—independent achievement supposedly ran counter to "women's nature." They did not exist apart from men. This attitude did not reflect women's reality, however, but rather represented the patriarchal ideal of womanhood. It benefited men to perceive women as primarily longing to love a man and be loved by him, to admire him and serve him, and even to pattern herself after him. Women's obvious dependency on men was not innate, however. It was learned. Women admired and served men not because that's their nature, but because tradition and male power shaped women's choices and behaviors.

"Women want a different kind of relationship with men and in the world but they feel resistance from both men and society."

Even today, views of a successful woman require that she attach to or depend on others—in particular, that she affiliate with and attach to a man. Many people wonder what good a career is to a woman if she has no one to come home to. Women without husbands evoke pity. Girls still learn from an early age that their main role is to attract men as life partners; containing or limiting their own achievement may become necessary if relationships with men become endangered. A competent, worldly, and ambitious woman could invite the kiss of death because such women are less desirable to men as life partners. Men ostensibly prefer women who need them.

A case in point is the Harvard-Yale study on the marriage prospects of women over 30. Although the motivations of the researchers remain unclear, no mention was made about attempts to gather parallel data on the marriage prospects of men over 30. The study, released in 1986, asserted, incorrectly as we will see later, that women who postpone marriage beyond their 20s may never find a mate. The study gave white, college-educated 30-year-old women just a 20% chance of marrying. Women at 35 were given a mere 5% chance; at 40, the odds dropped to 1.3%. For black women over 30, the odds were considered even dimmer.

These dismal prospects caused considerable hysteria among many women I know and even resulted in some women reconsidering their career decisions. One of my students, a single woman in her 30s, turned down a demanding position for one that would leave her more time for a social life. She heard this study reported on television and decided to maximize her availability. A 36-year-old colleague confided that the day she heard the report on the radio, she turned down an attractive offer that would have taken her out of a metropolitan area with a large professional population. She wondered later whether the statistics, which she intuitively knew could not be correct, had unconsciously influenced her decision: "I think I am beyond that. But the idea of never finding a mate really scares me and makes me angry at the same time. Wanting a relationship is natural. But the spotlight stays on women like me. If we never marry, people say it's our own fault. 'You made the wrong decision. Tough luck, lady.' It also galls me that anyone would conduct such a study. What's the point of it—to scare women into traditional roles?"

A later study by the Census Bureau differed with the Harvard-Yale predictions. Its calculations indicated that single 30-year-old women have a 58-66% chance of getting married. And at 40, the estimated chance was 17-23%. This later set of projections may or may not be accurate. Nevertheless, the societal message to women is loud and clear. Unlike men, women may not be able to have a career *and* a family. Developing a career, which may require postponing marriage, makes women *less* desirable as partners but renders men *more* desirable. Moreover, men can marry after 30 without worry. Their age does not necessarily jeopardize prospects of marrying and their biological clock with regard to childbearing ticks much longer.

Becoming Cinderella

The emotional upset caused by reports of the Harvard-Yale study caught some women by surprise. Was this sufficient reason to contemplate or reconsider career decisions? Did they have to give up their careers to get a man? Should they have married earlier and run the risk of not finishing school or establishing careers? Were they neurotically dependent on a man? Were they no different from Colette Downing, author of *The Cinderella Syndrome*, who nearly gave up her professional ambitions as a writer once a man slipped a gold ring on her left finger? She derived the title of her book from the prince's putting a glass slipper on Cinderella's left foot.

Such self-doubts arise as a result of female *and* male socialization. Women want a different kind of relationship with men and in the world but they feel resistance from both men and society. On the one hand, many women know careers and relationships fit for them. On the other hand, they wonder whether traditional views reflect some basic kernel of truth about women and men. The popular press and the general culture feed these doubts. . . .

Traditional Roles

Women often fall into traditional patterns with men without even realizing it. It is not unusual for women to enter into relationships with fairly "enlightened" men only to find that they have slipped into picking up dirty socks and worrying about meals while "he is out playing golf." Still today, women may consciously or unconsciously relinquish or hide their own strength and protect men from the knowledge that they can take care of themselves. Some fear, perhaps realistically, that women are less desired by men when they are economically independent and personally assertive. Reports like the Harvard-Yale study confirm their apprehensions.

"The notion that women must strengthen men by relinquishing or hiding their own strength is not new."

Consistent with female socialization, then, some women may assume a dependent stance in relationships with men as a way of having a career and family. This underfunctioning, which primarily serves to protect men from women's ability to act autonomously, also serves to protect women. That is, women may believe they need to subordinate themselves to men in physical and/or intellectual contexts regardless of their actual capabilities. By so doing, they can assure themselves a safe place with men. Because underfunctioning as a strategy has its roots in traditional aspects of female and male socialization, certain marital patterns may be unintentionally developed between partners without either partner recognizing what actually motivates his or her behavior. In one situation, for example, the wife handled all the finances, including investments and monthly bills, and routinely consulted with her husband on these matters. However, consistent with traditional views, they both saw him, not her, making the decisions about money.

Stroking the Male Ego

The notion that women must strengthen men by relinquishing or hiding their own strength is not new. We see poignant examples in fairy tales, movies, and real life. A vivid illustration of female underfunctioning occurs in the short story "Barcelona."

> The story describes Persis Fox, a "fairly successful illustrator" who is beginning to be sought after by New York publishers but sees herself as cowardly and fearful. Her husband Thad, in contrast, is a self-assured, self-directed, confident man who teaches at Harvard. The couple are on vacation in Barcelona and on their way to a remote restaurant when a thief suddenly snatches Persis's purse. Thad, who has been quite unattentive to Persis, suddenly springs into action and runs after the thief despite the darkness, danger, and unfamiliar terrain. The purse is recovered on the cobbles and the couple return to the restaurant.
>
> Thad asks, "Aren't you going to check it? See what's still there?"
>
> . . . "Oh good, my passport's still here," she tells Thad.
>
> "That's great." He is genuinely pleased with himself—and why should he not be, having behaved with such courage? Then he frowns. "He got all your money?"
>
> "Well, no, actually there wasn't any money. I keep it in my pocket. Always when I go to New York, that's what I do."
>
> Why does Thad look so confused just then? A confusion of emotions is spread across his fair, lined face. He is disappointed, somehow? Upset that he ran after a thief who had stolen a bag containing so little? Upset that Persis, who now goes down to New York on publishing business by herself, has tricks for self-preservation?
>
> "But you said your passport's still there?"
>
> "Oh yes, of course," Persis babbles. "That would have been terrible. We could have spent days in offices."
>
> Gratified, sipping at his wine, Thad says, "I wonder why he didn't take it, actually." Persis does not say, "Because it's hidden inside my address book"—although quite possibly that was the case. Instead, she says what is also surely true: "Because you scared him. The last thing he expected was someone running after him, and that *whistle*."
>
> Thad smiles and his face settles into a familiar expression: that of a generally secure, intelligent man, a lucky person, for whom things happen more or less as he would expect them to.

Thus, Persis protects Thad from the knowledge that his motivations for protecting her against worldly dangers are unfounded and that, in essence, she knows how to take care of herself. She also realizes that Thad's reasons for protecting her relate more to his needs than to her needs: In the story, Persis thinks, "He is not doing this [the chase] for her; it is something between men." They both collude to maintain a system that shelters the male ego from the threat of female competence and that continues an illusion of female dependency. Thad does not want to see Persis's recently developed independence and competence in dealing with the external world, and she makes little effort to show it to him.

The Costs of Compromise

Persis Fox's dilemma and insight parallel the experiences of many women in dual-career marriages. Some women may even recognize how they take a dependent stance with men but consider it necessary and useful. The tradeoff or cost, of course, entails taking a one-down position vis-à-vis the man. One woman reported that her husband complained about not feeling needed by her. She responded by centering her life around him more, which helped matters immeasurably from his perspective. In the process, however, she compromised egalitarian goals and even developed symptoms of depression.

Lucia A. Gilbert has written Men and Dual Career Families *and* Sharing It All.

"Feminists have . . . arrived at a view of men and masculinity that parallels the worst misogyny."

Men Are Victims of Sexism

Nicholas Davidson

Feminists have been all too successful in their efforts to create a "woman-centered" point of view. Freed from the check of men's input—just as misogynists in past centuries spouted their nonsense without fear of women's objections—they arrived at a view of men and masculinity that parallels the worst misogyny.

The qualities feminists impute to themselves are perversely reflected in their descriptions of men. Each female virtue is counterbalanced by an equivalent male vice: cooperation by competition, connectedness by separateness, pacifism by aggressivity, intuition by logic, until finally the feminist lexicon becomes a mirror image of the very prejudice against which it allegedly revolted.

There are two feminist mistakes here which it is important to explicitly refute. First, human temperament, though gendered, is not nearly as polarized as the feminist perspective requires it to be. Men and women resemble each other far more than one would expect from the feminist railing against the masculine traits. The second and more insidious mistake, because it jibes so neatly with the still-fashionable culturism of our time, concerns the exaggerated, stereotypical form in which the masculine traits are depicted in feminist texts: for these traits are in their real forms valuable and desirable, and are of basic importance to the emotional well-being and social utility of men.

But such caveats could not be made in the Feminist Era, when men learned that to express an opinion about gender to a feminist was to guarantee swift and shrill assault—not so much because of the specific opinion offered as because a "male" dared to offer an opinion at all. Poor shrimp! Didn't he realize that "feminism is humanism"?

Their opinions rejected, and being both despised and desired for their aggression and brawn, men were in a real sense reduced to sex objects. The man actually sought by heterosexual feminists is a brilliant provider and an aggressive but considerate lover who doesn't think too hard, at least not about matters of gender. He must combine the irreconcilable ideals of traditional masculinity and the New Male. He is expected to be dominant, but to believe he is living in sexual equality; to be rugged and independent, but to defer abjectly to feminism, no matter how completely feminists disagree with one another; to have a Stone Age sex drive and a modern age sense of guilt.

The objectification of men was reinforced by the use of "male" as a pejorative, and of "male" as a noun to be used in preference to "men," "husbands," or any less impersonal, distancing expressions. For instance, feminists criticize "*male*-centered" views in social science, but recommend "*woman*-centered" views as the alternative. Feminists prefer the word "male" to the word "man" because it is abstract and impersonal; it dulls the awareness in feminist proselytes that those being reviled and ridiculed are their fathers, brothers, lovers, and husbands.

Stereotyping Men

This usage of "male" drove home the perception of men as an "oppressor class." While complaining ceaselessly that men stereotyped women, feminists proceeded, with virtual unanimity, to stereotype men. Subtleties, qualifications, and diversities were ignored as feminists engaged in a general condemnation of "male aggression," "male dominance," "male violence," "male insensitivity," "male chauvinism," and so on. If it was true that "feminism is humanism," then women were the human sex; men, the inhuman one.

There are of course tactless, insensitive men who are inherently difficult to live with, who make

Reprinted from Nicholas Davidson's *The Failure of Feminism*, with permission of Prometheus Books, Buffalo, New York.

distant fathers and infuriating husbands. But the feminist perspective bloated the numbers of such types beyond all reasonable measure. Feminists typically came to believe that this stereotype applied to most or even to all men.

The Exceptions

Heterosexual feminists are constantly surprised that the particular man they love doesn't fit this repellent image. They describe him as a miracle, the one man among millions with whom they could bear to spend their time. Perhaps the most poignant comment on this belief is Nancy Chodorow's tribute to her lover in *The Reproduction of Mothering*:

> Michael Reich has been throughout this project unendingly encouraging. He has read and discussed with me at length countless drafts of sentences, paragraphs, and chapters, and the final product bears the mark of his careful and critical intellect. His supportiveness and nurturance undercut one main argument of this book.

They do indeed. What wistfulness, what unintended pathos is here as this major feminist theorist approaches the unbridgeable gap between feminist ideology and a woman's life.

Men in general continue to be lambasted by feminists without pity and, indeed, without any awareness of excess. It is commonly argued that men are "divorced from their emotions," that they find it hard to talk or even think about themselves or others except in abstract, impersonal terms. Yet this image, widely accepted in feminist writing, is no more than a caricature.

Exposing the Feminist Myth

Men are said to have difficulty talking about their feelings, but in general they know quite well what their feelings are. Men are equally as competent about human emotion as women, they are just less interested in spending equally large amounts of time bathing in it. The endless agonizing that occupies the diaries of adolescent girls seems incomprehensible and absurd to most men, who would rather be engaged in more productive, and to them more interesting, pursuits: Who is to say they are wrong?

The impersonal ordered hierarchies that men instantly establish in a group, which are so denigrated by feminists, present considerable advantages over the more personal groups in which the majority of women feel most comfortable. There is a real freedom in *not* caring about someone else's feelings, his opinion of you, and his relationships in general. "What does he think of me?" becomes much less important than "What can he do?" It is possible to concentrate on the task at hand, and actually, quite often, to "be oneself" far more than is the case if one must be constantly, primarily, concerned with the moment-to-moment evolution of emotional nuance.

Women do not understand themselves better than men. Nor are they more open. As a recent article points out, "Those supposedly open windows into the feminine heart are usually covered with drapes, curtains, fans, shades, gauze, screens, fog from fog machines and scrims of many colors."

Perhaps the supreme irony of feminism is that it led to a new exaggeration of gender difference. If women were to be praised for their sensitivity, men were to be condemned for their lack of it. Condemned to "insensitivity," the New Man was to passively await knowledge from feminists. "Sensitivity" became a patronizing compliment bestowed by feminists on men who submitted to the divorce from authenticity; it was passed off as the newest innovation for men. What about, one wondered, a Tolstoy? How could an "insensitive male" develop female characters with such deep resonance for so many women? What about the Jungian perception that insight into both sexes is inherent in the nature of each?

Men Should Not Change

In the endlessly conflicted amalgam of unisexism and female chauvinism that is feminism, one thing is consistent: the male is always guilty, and must change. But have women really changed, and should men change?

The Feminist Era left a whole cohort of women unmarried in their late twenties, thirties, and forties. Women, it was said in the seventies and early eighties, had become newly selective about men, who could not meet their justly high standards. By 1986, it had become apparent the tables were turned: that many women who were still unmarried by their late twenties were not going to find mates even if they wanted to. Men, it turns out, prefer to marry women who are younger than themselves; and a woman is at her peak of marriageability in her early twenties.

"Men . . . should not try to stop being men in order to become people with penises."

But as usual, feminists call on men to change. In the seventies, men were too "insensitive" for women to marry, in the eighties they are marrying the wrong women. If men are more attracted to younger women, there must be something wrong with them, since this preference is inconvenient for the acolytes of the role revolution. Why, though, should men change? Why shouldn't *women* change—change, that is, their life plans to include an earlier marriage, at the time when women are at their most powerful in sociobiological terms, the top echelon of society's "sexual aristocracy"?

Each stage of life should be accepted and enjoyed for what it is. But as usual, feminists prefer to advocate a wholesale remodeling of the human being, rather than to admit they have been in error, and seek simpler, more workable solutions to the adjustment of the sexes.

Feminists have endlessly condemned "male sexual aggression." But what really goes on in most sexual activity bears little relation to this blanket condemnation of men. The man initiates only after the woman has signaled that his advances will not be rejected. This simple, basic distinction is understood and respected by most people except feminists and rapists. Most male sexual aggression consists in taking the initiative, not in imposing one's will, and certainly not in a lack of consideration, let alone in violence: it is a matter of directing the show, not of engaging in either coercion or brutality (although a little symbolic coercion is keenly appreciated by most women, to feminists' perennial horror).

"Sex difference is apt to be a source of compatibility between men and women."

Given the tremendous ease with which men function as initiators in sex, and the satisfaction that women take in their reciprocal pattern, are we justified in changing so basic and congenial a modality? Do women really want men to change? In the case of lesbians, is it really appropriate that they concern themselves—as radical lesbian feminists endlessly have—with men's and heterosexual women's sexuality?

Men are criticized for their "separateness," which is unfavorably contrasted by Chodorow and others with women's "connectedness." But separateness and connectedness each have their advantages and pitfalls. Men's separateness appears to explain why, to their despair, most gay men are unable to form viable love relationships. Women's connectedness appears to explain why lesbians have no such difficulty. Lesbians' problem is different. A whole body of feminist literature has grown up around the theme of women's *inability* to separate from lesbian relationships, and from unsatisfactory relationships in general. The obvious conclusion is not that there is something wrong with either men or women, but rather that men and women function best together: that, for all the possibilities of misunderstanding which exist between men and women, heterosexual couples operate at a considerable advantage over homosexual ones; in short, that *men and women belong together just as they are.*

Men should not change: should not try to stop being men in order to become people with penises. It is not wrong for men to be masculine any more than it is for women to be feminine; it is not unnatural but natural. It is a waste of time to struggle to understand the New Woman for she does not really exist (not as she is supposed to be respected, at any rate). But men should study women as women, for the sexes are not alike and the understanding of each requires an effort from the other. Once women's general needs are grasped, most men are well able to meet them, for their own tendencies, while different, are complementary.

Beneficial Differences

For example, feminists and other moralizers often claim that men initially perceive attractive women as sex objects and that women initially perceive attractive men as potential partners in intimacy. This contrast is wildly exaggerated. But even if it were completely true, would it really matter? If men come to intimacy through sex and women come to sex through intimacy, that they travel by different paths is not important if they reach the same destination.

In fact, to the extent the sexes are different, they need each other's difference to become whole. It seems that every time a social critic, whether of the left or the right, notices yet another difference between the sexes, it is held up as yet further evidence of the fundamental incompatibility of men and women. The opposite would be far closer to the truth: that sex difference is apt to be a source of *compatibility* between men and women.

No doubt sex difference can also be a source of conflict and misunderstanding. But the difficulties caused by sex difference must not obscure its benefits. In their difference, the sexes do not conflict with so much as complete each other. The roots of this difference are set before birth and while men and women can and must learn from each other, there are sharp limits to the ability of any individual to assimilate both male and female styles. The attempt by either men or women to take over the other's frame of reference results in a sort of graceless behavioral transvestitism whose practitioners are constantly groping for elusive cues they don't really understand. It is a symptom of the impaired sexual constitution of our society that these facts, which are obvious, should seem outrageous.

A better consensus on gender must start from the premise that neither sex has anything to apologize for. In the Feminist Era, men and women were endlessly warned against the "traditional" characteristics of their sexes. Such pressures were misconceived at the outset and must be stopped. Boys at Concord Academy and young women at Barnard College don't need to hear yet more propaganda directed against the influence of biological gender, they need support for the gender they already have.

Nicholas Davidson writes for The Liberator, *a publication of Men's Rights Association.*

bibliography

The following bibliography of books, periodicals, and pamphlets is divided into chapter topics for the reader's convenience.

Child Care

Gary S. Becker — "Sure, Spend More on Child Care. But Spend Wisely," *Business Week*, May 8, 1989.

Allan Carlson — *Family Questions: Reflections on the American Social Crisis*. New Brunswick, NJ: Transaction Books, 1988.

Jaclyn Fierman — "Child Care: What Works—And Doesn't," *Fortune*, November 21, 1988.

Trish Hall — "Child Care, as Seen by Children," *The New York Times*, January 26, 1989.

Gwen Ifill — "Remembering the Children," *The Washington Post National Weekly Edition*, February 13-19, 1989.

William F. Jasper — "My Mother the State," *The New American*, January 30, 1989.

Tamar Lewin — "Small Tots, Big Biz," *The New York Times Magazine*, January 29, 1989.

Connaught Marshner — "Socialized Motherhood: As Easy as ABC," *National Review*, May 13, 1988.

A.P. Murphy — "Singing the Child Care Blues," *Parents*, February 1989.

The New Republic — "Bringing Up Baby," June 13, 1988.

Phyllis Schlafly — "The Child Care and Career Dilemmas," *The Phyllis Schlafly Report*, April 1989. Available from Box 618, Alton, IL 62002.

Lori Silver — "Full Child Support: Small Steps," *Los Angeles Times*, January 23, 1989.

Lena Williams — "Child Care at Job Site: Easing Fears," *The New York Times*, March 16, 1989.

Fern Winston — "Confronting Reality for Our Children," *People's Daily World*, January 24, 1989. Available from Long View Publishing Co., Inc., 239 W. 23rd St., New York, NY 10011.

Edward F. Zigler and Meryl Frank, eds. — *The Parental Leave Crisis: Toward a National Policy*. New Haven, CT: Yale University Press, 1988.

Family

Allan Carlson — *Family Questions: Reflections on the American Social Crisis*. New Brunswick, NJ: Transaction Books, 1988.

Allison Leigh Cowan — "'Parenthood II': The Nest Won't Stay Empty," *The New York Times*, March 12, 1989.

Creasie Finney Hairston and Peg McCartt Hess — "Family Ties," *Corrections Today*, April 1989.

William Gildea — "Father and Son," *Reader's Digest*, January 1989.

Herbert Gold — "Father Love," *American Health*, January/February 1989.

Daniel R. Harris — "Non-Nuclear Proliferation," *Utne Reader*, March/April 1989.

Norman M. Lobsenz — "Tips for Closer Family Ties," *Reader's Digest*, February 1989.

Connaught Marshner — "What Social Conservatives Really Want," *National Review*, September 2, 1988.

Elaine Tyler May — *Homeward Bound*. New York: Basic Books, 1988.

Daniel Morris — "Mom Liked You Best: How Christians Outgrow Sibling Rivalry," *U.S. Catholic*, January 1989.

Origins — "The Family," March 30, 1989. Available from National Catholic News Services, 1312 Massachusetts Ave. NW, Washington, DC 20005.

Norman Podhoretz — "The Family Idea Is Enjoying a New Life," *Conservative Chronicle*, October 12, 1988. Available from Box 29, Hampton, IA 50441.

Psychology Today — "The Benefits of Fatherhood," March 1989.

Brian Schofield-Bodt — "Paternity Leave as Church Praxis," *The Christian Century*, May 3, 1989.

Linda Lee Small — "A Piece of the Dream," *Ms.*, March 1988.

Feminism

America — "Doing Right by Women and the Trinity Too," February 11, 1989.

April Carter — *The Politics of Women's Rights*. New York: Longman, 1988.

Angela Y. Davis — *Women, Culture, and Politics*. New York: Random House, 1989.

Dinesh D'Souza — "Second Thoughts on Feminism," *Crisis*, February 1989. Available from the Brownson Institute, Inc., Box 1006, Notre Dame, IN 46556.

Mary Anne Dolan — "Feminism Failed," *The New York Times Magazine*, June 26, 1988.

Cynthia Fuchs Epstein — *Deceptive Distinctions*. New Haven, CT: Yale University Press, 1988.

Jeffrey P. Hart — ''Report from a Phallocrat,'' *National Review*, February 24, 1989.

Gertrude Himmelfarb — ''Self-Defeating Feminism,'' *The New York Times*, May 8, 1989.

Jill Lieber — ''The Woman Warrior,'' *Sports Illustrated*, February 1989.

Mary Ann Mason — *The Equality Trap*. New York: Simon & Schuster, 1988.

Henry Mohr — ''Women-in-Combat a Social Experiment,'' *Conservative Chronicle*, May 18, 1989. Available from Box 29, Hampton, IA 50441.

National Catholic Reporter — ''''Radical Feminism' Criticized,'' March 24, 1989.

Newsweek — ''Feminism and the Churches,'' February 13, 1989.

Letty Cottin Pogrebin — ''It Started with a Lunch,'' *Ms.*, January 1989.

Laurel Richardson and Verta Taylor, eds. — *Feminist Frontiers II*. New York: Random House, 1989.

Lindsy Van Gelder — ''It's Not Nice To Mess with Mother Nature,'' *Ms.*, January 1989.

Steven R. Weisman — ''Where Births Are Kept Down and Women Aren't,'' *The New York Times*, January 29, 1989.

Gretchen E. Ziegenhals — ''Digging in the Gardens of Feminist Theology,'' *Christian Century*, March 8, 1989.

Work

Randy Albelda — ''Women's Income Not up to Par,'' *Dollars & Sense*, July/August 1988.

Sharon Baker-Johnson — ''Working and Parenting: Can We Do Both?'' *Daughters of Sarah*, March/April 1988.

Aimee Lee Ball — ''Learning To Love Life at the Top,'' *Working Woman*, June 1989.

Aaron Bernstein — ''So You Think You've Come a Long Way, Baby?'' *Business Week*, February 29, 1988.

Beverly Beyette — ''A New Career Flap,'' *Los Angeles Times*, March 17, 1989.

Bryce Christensen et al. — *The Family Wage: Work, Gender, and Children in the Modern Economy*. Rockford, IL: The Rockford Institute, 1988.

Sherry Suib Cohen — *Tender Power*. Reading, MA: Addison-Wesley, 1989.

Elizabeth Ehrlich — ''The Mommy Track,'' *Business Week*, March 20, 1989.

Glamour — ''Will You Be Penalized for Having a Baby?'' February 1989.

Blythe Hamer — ''When the Boss Becomes Pregnant,'' *Psychology Today*, January/February 1989.

Barbara Kantrowitz — ''Advocating a 'Mommy Track,''' *Newsweek*, March 13, 1989.

Linda Lehrer — ''More than She Bargained for,'' *Ms.*, January/February 1989.

Dyan Machan — ''Taking Charge,'' *Forbes*, March 6, 1989.

Susan McHenry and Linda Lee Small — ''Does Part-Time Pay Off?'' *Ms.*, March 1989.

Mary Ann Mason — *The Equality Trap*. New York: Simon & Schuster, 1988.

Gretchen Morgenson — ''Sexual Harassment in the Workplace—Is It a Phony Issue?'' *Forbes*, May 15, 1989.

Beatrice Nivens — ''Managing Your Career and Family,'' *Essence*, January 1989.

Jeannie Ralston — ''When a Woman Does a 'Man's Job,''' *McCall's*, October 1988.

Anne M. Russel — ''The Tenth Annual Working Woman Salary Survey,'' *Working Woman*, January 1989.

Felice N. Schwartz — ''The 'Mommy Track' Isn't Anti-Woman,'' *The New York Times*, March 22, 1989.

USA Today — ''Keys to Women's Fulfillment,'' January 1989.

Richard K. Vedder — ''Shrinking Paychecks: The New Economics of Family Life,'' *The Family in America*, January 1989. Available from The Rockford Institute, PO Box 416, Mount Morris, IL 61054.

Angela Ward — ''A Feminist Mystique,'' *Newsweek*, September 12, 1988.

index